Robin Hood: The Earliest Ballads and Plays

Robin Hood
The Earliest Ballads and Plays

Edited with an introduction by

Charles Siegel

Omo Press

adolescentium alunt
senectutem oblectant

Sources of illustrations:

cover: N. C. Wyeth, illustrator, *Robin Hood* (1917)

p. 2: Late nineteenth century illustration, artist unknown

pp 5, 6: Lucy Fitch Perkins, *Robin Hood* (1923)

p. 16: A painting by John Gilbert made into an engraving by Ward Lock (1854)

p. 40: *The Noble Birth and Gallant Atchievements of that Remarkable Outlaw Robin Hood*, volume 2 of William Thoms, *Early English Prose Romances* (1858)

p. 114: Andrew Lang editor, H.J. Ford illustrator, The Story of Robin Hood and Other Tales of Adventure and Battle (1902)

All others from Howard Pyle. Some Merry Adventures of Robin Hood, of Great Renown in Sherwood Forest (1913)

ISBN 978-1-941667-35-4

Contents

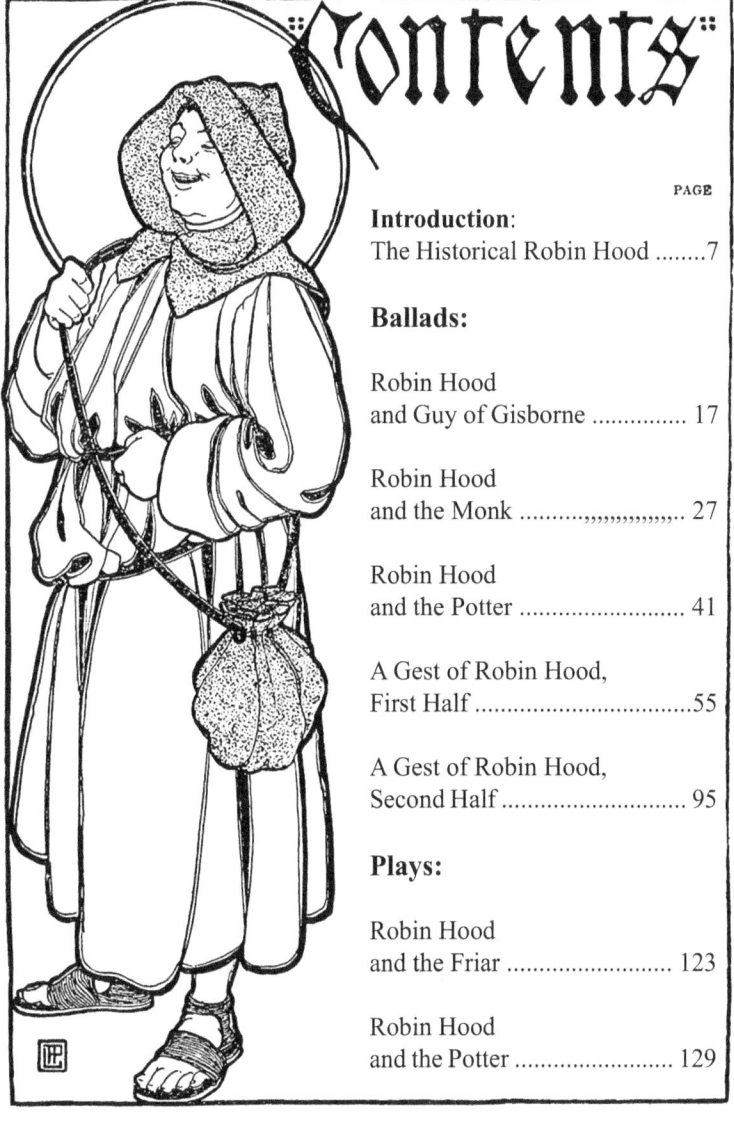

Come buy ye sweet ballads of bold ROBIN HOOD!

Introduction:
The Historical Robin Hood

The legends of Robin Hood began as popular ballads that spread as an oral tradition. The first reference to them in writing is in the famous book *Piers Plowman*, written in 1377, which says:

> I can noughte perfitly my pater-noster as the prest it syngeth,
> But I can rymes of Robyn Hood and Randalf erle of Chestre.

This quotation shows that the oral legend was already popular at this time. The Pater Noster, the Lord's Prayer in Latin, was known perfectly by priests who were educated, but the Robin Hood ballads in English were known by those who were less educated—and they must have been well known because they are one of only two sets of popular ballads that the quotation mentions.

The earliest written versions of the Robin Hood ballads that survive are from the later 1400s, about a century after *Piers Plowman*. The legends had been developing for some time before they were written down.

In addition to these ballads, there were folk dramas about Robin Hood, which became the standard entertainment during May Games in some places.

Before the Puritans abolished them in the seventeenth century, May Games lasted from May Day until Whitsuntide, the week following Whitsunday (the fiftieth day after Easter, also called Pentecost), which was a vacation week for peasants in medieval England. In medieval times, towns chose a May King and May Queen (or May Lord and May Lady) to rule over festivities that included dancing around the Maypole, sleeping in the woods, and contests in wrestling, archery, and other sports.

By the end of the fifteenth century, some towns replaced the May King and Queen with Robin Hood and Maid Marion, who led the festivities, while other legendary members of Robin Hood's band joined them. Aberdeen, Scotland, ordered in 1508 that "Robert huyd and litile Iohn" should lead the traditional May procession through town. In other places, the May King and Queen continued to lead, while Robin Hood and his band followed as part of the procession.

The festivities also included dramas about Robin Hood and his band. The complete text of one early play, "Robin Hood and the Friar," survives, and a fragment of another survives. The plays add some of the licentious character of the May festivities to the Robin Hood legends.

It is hard to place Robin Hood historically. The later version of the legend that has come down to our time says that he lived during the reign of King Richard the Lion Hearted and remained a loyal subject of the king but resisted his treacherous brother Prince John, who ruled while Richard was away fighting in the crusades and other foreign wars. But the earliest history books that mention Robin Hood place him at different times.

- **Andrew of Wyntoun's Orygynale Chronicle (c. 1420):** This history is sympathetic to William Wallace who fought for Scottish independence against King Edward I (reigned 1272-1307). He says that Little John and Robin Hood were two well-liked robbers in Inglewood and Barnesdale. Barnesdale is mentioned frequently in the Robin Hood ballads, but Inglewood is not, and it seems the historian added it because it is near the Scottish border and connects Robin Hood with the Scottish rebels.

- **Walter Bower's Continuation of John Fordun's Scotichronicon** (c. 1440): This history associates Robin Hood with the Barons led by Simon de Montfort who rebelled against Henry III (reigned 1216 – 1272). This Second Baron's War limited the power of the king and increased the power of parliament, and it is considered an important part of the history of England's constitution.

- **John Major's Historia Majoris Brittaniae (1521):** This later history is the first that puts Robin Hood in the time of King Richard the Lion Hearted (reigned 1189-1999), whose brother reigned as King John from 1199-1216, at the time of the First Baron's War, which forced King John to protect the rights of the Barons by issuing the Magna Carta, another landmark in the development of England's constitution. This history also says that Robin was a humane robber and a protector of women and the poor, as some of the earliest ballads imply.
- **Richard Grafton's Chronicle at Large (1569):** This later history summarized Major's history and also said Robin Hood was either an earl or a soldier who became an earl, but then had to become an outlaw after losing his wealth through wastefulness. Some later works use this idea that Robin was a nobleman, such as Anthony Munday's play *The Downfall of Robert, Erle of Huntington* (1598), but all the early ballads included in this book say that he was a yeoman and not a nobleman, as do most of the later legends.

It seems that, because Robin Hood was an outlaw and therefore an enemy of the King, the histories associated him with their own favorite rebels against the King, whether the barons rebelling against King John (1199-1216), the barons rebelling against Henry III (1216 – 1272), or William Wallace rebelling against Edward I (1272-1307). The historians pushed him further back in history one generation at a time, and the legend that has come down to us about his living in the time of King John is the latest version of his place in history.

These histories do not help us place the historical Robin Hood, but we can learn something from the ballads and plays. The image of Robin Hood in the legends changed over time, and this book contains only the earliest surviving versions, which can help us track down the historical Robin Hood.

There is evidence in the ballads that the Robin Hood legends originated later than any of the historians said. The historians place him between the time of King John and Edward I, but the earliest ballads place him at the time of Edward III, who reigned from 1327 to 1377. This is as late as he could have lived, since Piers Plowman mentioned the ballads in 1377.

Two ballads, "Robin Hood and the Monk" and "A Gest of Robin Hood" mention "our comely king." In addition to using the phrase several times, the Gest says explicitly "Edward, our comely king" at the end of Fitt 6. The word "comely" was a common description of King Edward IV (1461-1483), who was known for being handsome, and was also used of Edward III (1327-1377). The "Gest" also says that, when the king identified himself, he took out "the broad targe," and the Oxford English Dictionary tells us that "targe" was "a name applied in the reigns of the first three Edwards to the King's private or privy seal." The use of both words, "comely" and "targe," narrows it down to the time of Edward III. Of course, Robin also cannot be dated to the days of the comely Edward IV because he reigned after *Piers Plowman* mentioned the Robin Hood ballads.

The word "comely" is just used in two ballads, and it could have been used because the ballad was composed at the time of Edward III rather than because Robin Hood lived at that time. But other features that are pervasive in the ballads are also evidence of this late origin.

The solidly English names in all the ballads are evidence for this time of origin. After the Norman invasion in 1066, England spoke two languages, the Norman French of the conquerors, and the Anglo-Saxon of the conquered. For many generations, Norman French continued to be the language of the king and aristocrats descended from the conquerors: we can see it in names like Richard Coeur de Lion (around the time of King John and the first Baron's rebellion) and Simon de Montfort (who led the second Baron's rebellion). French was spoken in court at this time, and English did not become the language of the court until the time of Edward III. None of the characters in the Robin Hood legends have French names, including the knight Sir Richard at the Lee in "The Gest of Robin Hood." By contrast, the Arthurian legends include British names like Sir Ywaine and French names like Sir Lancelot du Lac, showing that this legend dates back to the time before the Anglo-Saxon conquest and other stories were added by the French. The characters in the Robin Hood ballads and legends are not Normans and Saxons; they are English, which places them in the time of Edward III, when the king, aristocrats, and commoners finally saw themselves as English rather than Normans and Saxons.

The economic class of the characters also fits in with the political conflicts at this later time of origin. In the days of the First and Second Baron's rebellion, the conflict was between the two powers of feudal society, the king and the barons, but the ballads say very clearly that Robin Hood and his men were yeomen.

This word's meaning changed over time. It seems that it always referred to a class of people who were above peasants and menial servants and below the gentry (large land owners) and nobles. The word "yeoman" originally referred to servants at this respectable social level; for example, the "yeomen of the guard" served this king but were not menials. Later, the word also came to mean an independent farmer who owned at least 100 acres of land but not as much land as the gentry. This meaning seems most relevant to the Robin Hood legends, since Robin Hood was independent and was no one's servant, his men were independent and voluntarily took him as their leader. The ballad of "Robin Hood and the Potter also calls the potter a yeoman and he was an independent craftsman and no one's servant. According to the *Oxford English Dictionary*, the first written use of "yeoman" to mean independent farmer rather than servant was in 1411—after the end of Edward III's reign. The only explanation for its frequent use in the Robin Hood ballads, which Piers Plowman mentioned in 1372, is that was used in popular speech to refer to someone who was not a servant earlier than its first written appearance.

The independent yeoman was an attractive symbol during the reign of Edward III because of the political conflicts that were going on at the time. In 1327, Edward II was forced to abdicate because he was unsuccessful at defending England from invasion, and parliament legitimized Edward III as his successor, establishing the importance of parliament in the English constitution. At the time, the commons, representing knights and burgesses, the free men of the towns, was part of parliament but the nobility, clergy, and commons met together, and kings sometimes called the commons only when they were needed and then sent them home again, In 1341, commons met separately from the nobility and clergy for the first time, and it continued to gain power during the rest of the reign of Edward III, establishing the principle that no tax could be levied or law passed without the consent of the king and both houses of parliament, which gave the commons its own share in government for the first time. In 1376, the year before Edward III's death, during the so-called "Good Parliament," the commons demanded an accounting of the king's spending and impeached some of the king's ministers; as a result, the king arrested the speaker of the House of Commons, who was released after the king's death.

Clearly, the main political struggle during of Edward's reign involved the commons, representatives of the knights and the independent merchants and craftsmen from the towns, asserting their power against the king, nobility and clergy. In the early legends, Robin Hood is allied with a potter (an independent craftsman) and a knight. In the "Gest of Robin Hood," he tells his men:

But look ye do no husband [farmer] harm,
That tilleth with his plough.
No more ye shall no good yeoman
That walketh by green wood shawe [grove],
Ne no knight ne no squire
That will be a good fellow.
These bishops and these archbishops,
Ye shall them beat and bind;
The high sheriff of Nottingham,
Him hold ye in your mind.

The "Gest" is the beginning of the later legend that Robin Hood robbed from the rich and gave to the poor, but in addition to the poor, he includes the knights among those he protects, while he robs from the wealthy clergy and the feudal hierarchy represented by the sheriff of Nottingham. In addition to the poor, he favors the classes represented in the House of Commons and opposes the king and classes represented in the House of Lords.

Scholars dispute where Robin Hood lived as well as when he lived. The ballads say he lived in Sherwood Forest near Barnesdale and harassed the Sheriff of Nottingham. There are two

Barnesdales in England, one in Yorkshire north of Nottingham and one in Rutland south of Nottingham. Though the Barnesdale in Rutland had what they called the "Robin Hood's Cave" before the cave was covered by a reservoir in 1975, the ballads refer to the Barnesdale in Yorkshire. In the "Gest of Robin Hood," for example, Robin tells his men to go into Barnesdale

And walk up to the Saylis,

And so to Watlinge Street,

which are places in the Barnesdale in Yorkshire.

Barnesdale is about fifty miles from Nottingham. Some scholars, beginning with Francis James Child who collected early English ballads during the second half of the 19th century, have argued that this was a long distance to travel and that Barnesdale was outside of the sheriff's jurisdiction because it was not in the shire of Nottingham, so they conclude that the Robin Hood legend must combine earlier legends about two outlaws, one in Barnesdale and one in Nottingham. Actually, fifty miles is about the limit of how far you can travel on horseback in one day. It makes sense that an outlaw would choose to live in a forest near Barnesdale, where law enforcement was apparently so weak that he could easily take money from people who passed through the forest, and that he would also go to rob in Nottingham occasionally, setting up a conflict between himself and the sheriff. It seems plausible that the legends were based on one outlaw who lived and robbed bypassers in the forest near Barnesdale, and who occasionally went to Nottingham, where there was more wealthy people to rob.

Though most clues in the ballads date the historic Robin Hood to the time of Edward III (1327-1377), there are also a few clues in the ballads that point to a much earlier origin to the Robin Hood legends. The most obvious is in the ballad "Robin Hood and Guy of Gisborne," which includes a fight based on an ancient pre-Christian ritual where the dominant male dresses as an animal and another male challenges him and tries to kill him. Of course, the May plays also include older elements, which have led some scholars to speculate that Robin Hood is based on Robin Goodfellow (Shakespeare's Puck), the son of Oberon, King of the Fairies. But it is unlikely that the Robin Hood legend would derive from these older legends without keeping some of the older names, as the Arthurian legend did. It is much more plausible that the Robin Hood legend began in the days of Edward III and that the new Robin Hood ballads incorporated bits of ancient ballads that had already been popular for a long time.

If so, it is striking how quickly the legend developed. Edward III reigned from 1327 to 1377, and the same year that his reign ended, *Piers Plowman* mentioned Robin Hood ballads as one of two examples of popular ballads. The most plausible explanation for the legend developing so quickly is that there actually was a band of outlaws living in the forest near Barnesdale, who sometimes raided Nottingham and provoked the sheriff there. Whenever there were new rumors about their activities, people wanted to know more about them, and the balladeers were glad to accommodate by inventing legends about them.

The legends became so popular because they were very appealing at a time when the knights and burgers were struggling against the king, lords and church to have some voice in governing themselves and to free themselves from oppressive medieval laws. When they were struggling to change the laws, it must have been a relief to fantasize about a band of independent yeoman who simply ignored the laws and governed themselves, living by poaching the king's deer and robbing the rich. Robin's men lived in the country, not the towns, but independent yeomen were an apt symbol of the independent burgesses of the towns. They chose their own leader by consent, as the burgers chose their representatives to parliament: at the end of Robin Hood and the Monk, Robin says that Little John should lead the group, but the men affirm that Robin should continue to lead.

Despite the early historians' attempts to connect them with earlier rebellions, the earliest legends clearly do not reflect the divisions between England and Scotland at the time of William Wallace, and do not reflect the divisions between the King and the Barons at the time of King Henry III and King John. They do reflect the social divisions between the commons and the king, nobles, and clergy in England at the time of Edward III, which explains why they became so popular so quickly at that time.

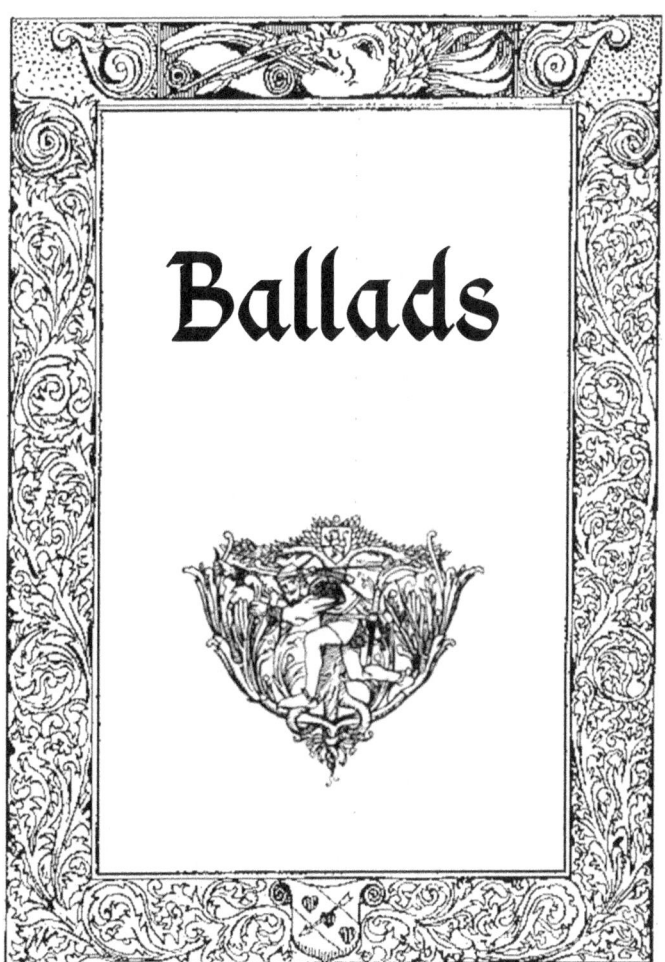

Ballads

Robin Hood and Guy of Gisborne

Some scholars have suggested that this ballad is the closest thing we have to the earliest Robin Hood legends, because it contains elements of ritual and magic. More likely, it is a story from an ancient ballad that was combined with a story from the newly popular ballads about Robin Hood.

Robin has a dream that two yeoman beat him. He and Little John go out looking for revenge and find Guy of Gisborne dressed in a horsehide, tail and mane. Little John volunteers to talk with him, and Robin is so insulted by the idea that he himself would not talk that he quarrels with Little John, who leaves him and goes to Barnesdale, where the sheriff captures and plans to hang him. Robin Hood fights with and kills Guy of Gisborne, cuts off his head, mutilates the face so it is unrecognizable, and he dresses in Guy's horse costume. Robin goes to Barnesdale to save Little John, and the sheriff thinks he is Guy because of the way he is dressed, so he is able to untie Little John and give him a bow, which Little John uses to kill the sheriff.

There is a reminiscence here of a pre-Christian ritual where the dominant male dresses as an animal and fights to defend his dominance. Anyone who beats him puts on the animal costume and assumes the identity of dominant male, mutilating his predecessor's face to destroy his identity completely. The conflation of dream and reality at the beginning of the ballad also shows a mythic origin.

Some scholars have said that some text must be missing from this ballad, because Robin Hood must have learned somehow that Little John was captured before going to save him. But in sort of mythic context, it is plausible that Robin knew it intuitively—as he went to search for Guy based on a dream.

The behavior from a forgotten ritual, presumably preserved in ancient ballads by people who no longer remembered the ritual itself, is combined with a typical story of Robin Hood and Little John quarrelling, the sheriff capturing one of them, and the other saving him.

This ballad survives in a mid-seventeenth century manuscript, now in the British Library, that was once owned by Thomas Percy, who published Reliques of Ancient English Poetry in 1765. Percy himself recognized that this ballad had "marks of much greater antiquity than any of the common popular songs on this subject."

When shawes been sheene and shradds* full fair,   [shawes been
And leaves both large and long,   sheene = groves
It is merry, walking in the fair forest,   are bright]
To hear the small birds sing.

The woodweel sang, and would not cease,   [woodweel = oriole]
Amongst the leaves a lyne.   [a lyne = of linden trees]
"And it is by two wight yeoman,   [wight = strong]
By dear God, that I mean.

Me thought they did me beat and bind,
And took my bow me fro;   [fro = from]
If I be Robin alive in this land,
I'll be wrocken on both them two."   [wrocken = revenged]

"Sweavens are swift, master," quoth John,   [sweavens = dreams]
"As the wind that blows o'er a hill,
For if it be never so loud this night,
Tomorrow it may be still."   [still = silent]

"Buske ye, bowne ye, my merry men all,   [buske = hurry,
For John shall go with me,   bowne = get ready]
For I'll go seek yond wight yeomen   [wight = strong]
In greenwood where they be."

---

* The word "shradds" seems to be corruption in the manuscript, which no one has
  been able to correct.

They cast on their gown of green,
A shooting gone are they,
Until they came to the merry greenwood,
Where they had gladdest be;
There were they ware of wight yeoman,   [wight = strong]
His body leaned to a tree.

A sword and a dagger he wore by his side,
Had been many a man's bane,
And he was clad in his capull-hide,   [capull = horse]
Top, and tail, and mane.

"Stand you still, master," quoth Little John,
"Under this trusty tree,
And I will go to yond wight yeoman,
To know his meaning truly."

"Ah, John, by me thou sets no store,
And that's a farley thing;   [farley = amazing]
How oft send I my men before,
And tarry myself behind?

It is no cunning a knave to ken,   [it takes no skill to know a knave]
An a man but hear him speak;   [an = if]
An it were not for bursting of my bow,
John, I would thy head break."

But often words they breeden bale, [breeden bale = cause evil]
That parted Robin and John;
John is gone to Barnesdale,
The gates he knows each one.

And when he came to Barnesdale,
Great heaviness there he had;   [heaviness = sadness]
He found two of his own fellows
Were slain both in a slade,   [slade = glade]

And Scarlett* afoot flying was,
Over stocks and stone,
For the sheriff with seven score men
Fast after him is gone.

"Yet one shot I'll shoot," says Little John,
"With Christ his might and main;
I'll make yond fellow that flies so fast
To be both glad and fain."

John bent up a good yew bow,
And fetteled him to shoot;   [fettled him = prepared himself]
The bow was made of a tender bough,
And fell down to his foot.†

"Woe worth thee, wicked wood," said Little John,
"That e're thou grew on a tree!
For this day thou art my bale,   [bale = evil]
My boot when thou should be!"   [boot = benefit]

This shot it was but loosely shot,
The arrow flew in vain,   [in vain = inaccurately]
And it met one of the sheriff's men;
Good William a Trent was slain.

It had been better for William a Trent
To hang upon a gallow
Then for to lie in the greenwood,
There slain with an arrow.

And it is said, when men be met,
Six can do more than three:
And they have tane Little John,   [tane = taken]
And bound him fast to a tree.

* Will Scarlett, who is called Will Scarlock in most early ballads.

† The bow broke when he shot.

"Thou shalt be drawn by dale and down," quoth the sheriff, [drawn
"And hanged high on a hill."   = dragged]
"But thou may fail," quoth Little John,
"If it be Christ's own will."

Let us leave talking of Little John,
For he is bound fast to a tree,
And talk of Guy and Robin Hood,
In the green wood where they be.

How these two yeomen together they met,
Under the leaves of lyne,   [lyne = linden tree]
To see what merchandise they made   [merchandise = business]
Even at that same time.

"Good morrow, good fellow," quoth Sir Guy;
"Good morrow, good fellow," quoth he,
"Methinks by this bow thou bearest in thy hand,
A good archer thou seems to be."

"I am willful of my way," quoth Sir Guy,   [willful = uncertain]
"And of my morning tide."   [tide = time]
"I'll lead thee through the wood," quoth Robin,
"Good fellow, I'll be thy guide."

"I seek an outlaw," quoth Sir Guy,
"Men call him Robin Hood;
I had rather meet with him upon a day,
Then forty pound of gold."

"If you two met, it would be seen whether were better   [whether
Afore ye did part away;   = which]
Let us some other pastime find,
Good fellow, I thee pray.

"Let us some other masteries make,   [masteries = tests of skill]
And we will walk in the woods even;
We may chance meet with Robin Hood
At some unset steven."   [unset steven = unexpected occasion]

They cut them down the summer shroggs   [shroggs = bushes]
Which grew both under a briar,
And set them three score rod* in twain,   [in twain = apart]
To shoot the pricks full near.

"Lead on, good fellow," said Sir Guy,   [lead on = shoot first]
"Lead on, I do bid thee."
"Nay, by my faith," quoth Robin Hood,
"The leader thou shalt be."

The first good shot that Robin led
Did not shoot an inch the prick fro;   [the prick fro = from the target]
Guy was an archer good enough,
But he could ne'er shoot so.

The second shot Sir Guy shot,
He shot within the garland;   [garland = ring hanging from
But Robin Hood shot it better than he,   a stick, used as a target]
For he clove the good prick-wand.   [split the stick that held the ring]

"God's blessing on thy heart!" says Guy,
"Good fellow, thy shooting is good,
For an thy heart be as good as thy hands,   [an = if]
Thou were better then Robin Hood.

"Tell me thy name, good fellow," quoth Guy,
"Under the leaves of lyne."   [lyne = linden tree]
"Nay, by my faith," quoth good Robin,
"Till thou have told me thine."

"I dwell by dale and down," quoth Guy,
"And I have done many a curst turn;   [curst turn = evil deed]
And he that calls me by my right name
Calls me Guy of good Gisborne."
"My dwelling is in the wood," says Robin,
"By thee I set right naught;
My name is Robin Hood of Barnesdale,
A fellow thou has long sought."

* Three score (60) rods = 330 feet.

He that had neither been a kith nor kin
Might have seen a full fair sight,
To see how together these yeomen went,
With blades both brown and bright.

To have seen how these yeomen together fought,
Two hours of a summer's day;
It was neither Guy nor Robin Hood
That fettled them to fly away.   [fettled them = prepared himself]

Robin was reckless on a root,   [reckless = careless]
And stumbled at that tide,   [tide = time]
And Guy was quick and nimble with-all,
And hit him o'er the left side.

"Ah, dear Lady!" said Robin Hood,
"Thou art both mother and may!   [may = maid]
I think it was never man's destiny
To die before his day."

Robin thought on Our Lady dear,
And soon leaped up again,
And thus he came with an awkward stroke;   [awkward = backhanded]
Good Sir Guy he has slain.

He took Sir Guy's head by the hair,
And sticked it on his bow's end:
"Thou hast been traitor all thy life,
Which thing must have an end."

Robin pulled forth an Irish knife,
And nicked Sir Guy in the face,
That he was never on a woman born   [so that no one born of woman]
Could tell who Sir Guy was.

Says, "Lie there, lie there, good Sir Guy,
And with me be not wroth;
If thou have had the worse strokes at my hand,
Thou shalt have the better cloth."

Robin did his gown of green,
On Sir Guy it throw;
And he put on that capull-hide,   [capull = horse]
That clad him top to toe.

"The bow, the arrows, and little horn,
And with me now I'll bear;
For now I will go to Barnesdale,
To see how my men do fare."

Robin set Guy's horn to his mouth,
A loud blast in it he did blow;
That beheard the sheriff of Nottingham,
As he leaned under a lowe.   [lowe = hill]

"Hearken! hearken!" said the sheriff,
"I heard no tidings but good,
For yonder I hear Sir Guy's horn blow,
For he hath slain Robin Hood.

"For yonder I hear Sir Guy's horn blow,
It blows so well in tide,   [well in tide = at a good time]
For yonder comes that wight yeoman,   [wight = strong]
Clad in his capull-hide.

"Come hither, thou good Sir Guy,
Ask of me what thou wilt have."
"I'll none of thy gold," says Robin Hood,
"Nor I'll none of it have."

"But now I have slain the master," he said,
"Let me go strike the knave;*
This is all the reward I ask,
Nor no other will I have."

"Thou art a madman," said the sheriff,

---

* Robin Hood, disguised as Guy of Gisborne, says that he has killed Robin Hood and wants to kill Little John.

"Thou shouldst have had a knight's fee;
Seeing thy asking be so bad,   [thy asking be so bad =
Well granted it shall be."   you have asked so little]

But Little John heard his master speak,
Well he knew that was his steven;   [steven = voice]
"Now shall I be loosed," quoth Little John,
"With Christ's might in heaven."

But Robin he hied him towards Little John,   [hied him = went]
He thought he would loose him belive;   [belive = immediately]
The sheriff and all his company
Fast after him did drive.

"Stand aback! stand aback!" said Robin;
"Why draw you me so near?
It was never the use in our country
One's shrift another should hear."   [shrift = confession before dying]

But Robin pulled forth an Irish knife,
And loosed John hand and foot,
And gave him Sir Guy's bow in his hand,
And bade it be his boot.   [boot = benefit]

But John took Guy's bow in his hand
His arrows were rusty by the root;
The sheriff saw Little John draw a bow
And fettle him to shoot.   [fettle him = prepare himself]

Towards his house in Nottingham
He fled full fast away,
And so did all his company,
Not one behind did stay.

But he could neither so fast go,
Nor away so fast run,
But Little John, with an arrow broad,
Did cleave his heart in twain.

The · Sheriff · of · Nottingham · cometh before · the · King · at · London

Robin Hood and the Monk

Conflicts for dominance between Robin Hood and Little John are common in the ballads collected in this book: they quarrel in this ballad, in "Robin Hood and Guy of Gisborne" and in "A Gest of Robin Hood," In other ballads, Robin quarrels with others who become his companions after putting up a good fight.

In this ballad, Robin Hood wants to go to Nottingham to pray during Whitsuntide. Little John joins Robin so he can help defend him from the sheriff, but they soon begin to quarrel. Little John says they should have an archery contest for pennies to pass time along the way, but Robin thinks he is so much better than John that he gives him three to one odds and soon loses five shillings (sixty pennies). When Robin says that John is lying about how much he owes, John leaves him. Robin Hood is captured and imprisoned in Nottingham after a monk sees him in the church and tells the sheriff. But Little John very cleverly deceives the monk, the king, and the Sheriff and frees Robin Hood.

In this ballad, Little John does better than Robin Hood, both as an archer and as a trickster who outwits the sheriff, but at the end, Robin offers to make Little John the head of his band, and John says that Robin should remain head. We can see that his men voluntarily accept Robin Hood as their leader.

Note that this ballad is similar to "Robin Hood and Guy of Gisborne," but the roles there are reversed: after they quarrel, Little John is captured and Robin rescues him.

This poem has been preserved in a manuscript owned by Cambridge University, which was written after 1450, which is probably the earliest written version of a Robin Hood ballad that survives.

In summer, when the shawes be sheene,   [shawes be sheyne =
And leaves be large and long,   groves are bright]
It is full merry in fair forest
To hear the fowls' song,   [fowls = birds]

To see the deer draw to the dale,
And leave the hills high,
And shadow them in the leaves green,
Under the greenwood tree.

It befell on Whitsuntide
Early in a May morning,
The sun up fair can shine,
And the birds merry can sing.

"This is a merry morning," said Little John,
"By Him that died on tree;   [tree = cross]
A more merry man then I am one
Lives not in Christianity.

"Pluck up thy heart, my dear master,"
Little John can say,
"And think it is a full fair time
In a morning of May."

"Yea, one thing grieves me," said Robin,
"And does my heart much woe:
That I may not no solemn day
To mass nor matins go.

"It is a fortnight and more," said he,
"Since I my Savior see;
Today will I to Nottingham," said Robin,
"With the might of mild Mary."

Than spoke Much, the miller's son,
Evermore well him betide!
"Take twelve of thy wight yeomen,   [wight = strong]

Well weaponed, by thy side.
Such one would thyself slon   [thyself slon = kill you if
That twelve dare not abide."   you were by yourself]

"Of all my merry men," said Robin,
"By my faith I will none have,
But Little John shall bear my bow,
Till that me list to draw."   [me list = I wish]

"Thou shall bear thine own," said Little John,
"Master, and I will bear mine,   [shoot a penny = shoot
And we will shoot a penny," said Little John,   arrows for a penny bet]
Under the green wood lyne."   [lyne = linden trees]

"I will not shoot a penny," said Robin Hood,
"In faith, Little John, with thee,
But ever for one as thou shoot," said Robin,
"In faith I hold thee three."*

Thus shot they forth, these yeomen two,
Both at bush and broom
Till Little John won of his master
Five shillings to hose and shoon.   [hose = socks; shoon = shoes]

A ferly strife fell them between,   [ferly = astonishing]
As they went by the way;
Little John said he had won five shillings,
And Robin Hood said shortly, nay.

With that Robin Hood lied Little John,   [lied = called a liar]
And smote him with his hand;
Little John waxed wroth therewith,   [waxed wroth = grew angry]
And pulled out his bright brand.   [brand = sword]

"Were thou not my master," said Little John,
"Thou shouldst be hit full sore;

* I will bet three pennies against your one.

Get thee a man where thou will,
For thou getst me no more."

Then Robin goes to Nottingham,
Him self morning alone,
And Little John to merry Sherwood,
The paths he knew ilkone.   [ilkone = each one]

When Robin came to Nottingham,
Certainly withouten layn,   [withouten layn = without lying]
He prayed to God and mild Mary
To bring him out safe again.

He goes in to Saint Mary church,
And kneeled down before the rood;   [rood = cross]
All that ever were the church within
Beheld well Robin Hood.

Beside him stood a great-headed monk,
I pray to God woe he be!
Full soon he knew good Robin,
As soon as he him see.

Out at the door he ran,
Full soon and anon;   [anon = soon]
All the gates of Nottingham
He made to be sparred everyone.   [sparred = barred]

"Rise up," he said, "thou proud sheriff,
Buske thee and make thee bowne;   [buske = hurry; bowne = ready]
I have spied the king's felon,
Forsooth he is in this town.

"I have spied the false felon,
As he stands at his mass;
It is long of thee," said the monk,   [long of thee = your fault]
"An ever he from us pass.   [an = if]

"This traitor name is Robin Hood,
Under the greenwood lynd;   [lynd = linden trees]
He robbed me once of a hundred pound,
It shall never out of my mind."

Up then rose this proud sheriff,
And radly made him yare;   [radly = quickly; yare = ready]
Many was the mother son
To the kirk with him can fare.   [can fare = went]

In at the doors they throly thrast,   [throly thrast = boldly pushed]
With staves full good wone;   [full good wone = many]
"Alas, alas!" said Robin Hood,
"Now miss I Little John."

But Robin took out a two-hand sword,
That hanged down by his knee;
There as the sheriff and his men stood thickest
Thitherward would he.

Thrice through at them he ran then,
Forsooth as I you say,
And wounded many a mother son,
And twelve he slew that day.

His sword upon the sheriff head
Certainly he brake in two;
"The smith that thee made," said Robin,
"I pray to God work him woe!

"For now am I weaponless," said Robin,
"Alas! against my will;
But if I may flee these traitors from,   [but if = unless]
I wot they will me kill."   [wot = know]

Robin into their church ran,
Throughout them everilkon,   [everilkon = every one]

*[Gap in the text. Robin Hood is captured and jailed, and the
Sheriff of Nottingham sends the monk to the king to have Robin
executed. Little John tells Robin Hood's men this news.]*

Some fell in swooning as they were dead,
And lay still as any stone;
None of them were in their mind
But only Little John.

"Let be your rule," said Little John,   [rule = moaning]
"For His love that died on tree,   [tree = cross]
Ye that should be doughty men;
It is great shame to see.

"Our master has been hard bestode   [hard bestode = hard pressed]
And yet scaped away;
Pluck up your hearts, and leave this moan,
And hearken what I shall say.

"He has served Our Lady many a day,
And yet will, securely;
Therefore I trust in her specially
No wicked death shall he die.

"Therefore be glad," said Little John,
"And let this mourning be;
And I shall be the monk's guide,
With the might of mild Mary,

An I meet him," said Little John   [an = if]
"We will go but we two.
*[Small gap in text:
Little John will go with Much the miller's son.]*

"Look that ye keep well our tristil tree,   [tristil = meeting]
Under the leaves small,
And spare none of this venison,
That goes in this vale."

Forth then went these yemen two,
Little John and Much on fere,   [on fere = together]
And looked on Much emys house;   [looked on=stopped at;
The highway lay full near.   emys = uncle's]

Little John stood at a window in the morning,
And looked forth at a stage;
He was ware where the monk came riding,   [ware = aware]
And with him a little page.

"By my faith," said Little John to Much,
"I can thee tell tidings good;
I see where the monk comes riding,
I know him by his wide hood."

They went in to the way, these yemen both,
As courteous men and hende;   [hende = courteous]
They spyrred tidings at the monk,   [spyrred tidings = asked for news]
As they had been his friend.

"From whence come ye?" said Little John,
"Tell us tidings, I you pray,
Of a false outlaw,
Was taken yesterday.

"He robbed me and my fellows both
Of twenty mark in certain;
If that false outlaw be taken,
Forsooth we would be fain."   [fain = glad]

"So did he me," said the monk,
Of a hundred pound and more;
I laid first hand him upon,
Ye may thank me therefore."

"I pray God thank you," said Little John,
"And we will when we may;
We will go with you, with your leave,

And bring you on your way.

"For Robin Hood has many a wild fellow,
I tell you in certain;
If they wist ye rode this way,   [wist = knew]
In faith ye should be slain."

As they went talking by the way,
The monk and Little John,
John took the monk's horse by the head,
Full soon and anon.   [anon = soon]

John took the monk's horse by the head,
Forsooth as I you say;
So did Much the little page,
For he should not scape away.

By the gullet of the hood   [gullet = neck]
John pulled the monk down;
John was nothing of him agast,   [agast = afraid]
He let him fall on his crown.

Little John was so aggrieved,
And drew out his sword in high;
The monk saw he should be dead,
Loud mercy can he cry.

"He was my master," said Little John,
"That thou hast brought in bale;   [bale = harm]
Shall thou never come at our king,
For to tell him tale."

John smote off the monk's head,
No longer would he dwell;
So did Much the little page,
For fear lest he would tell.

There they buried them both,

In neither moss nor lyng,   [lyng = bush]
And Little John and Much in fere   [in fere = together]
Bare the letters to our king.

Little John came in unto the king
He kneeled down upon his knee:
"God you save, my liege lord,
Jesus you save and see!

"God you save, my liege king!"
To speak John was full bold;
He gave him the letter in his hand,
The king did it unfold.

The king read the letters anon,   [anon = soon]
And said, "So mot I the,   [mot I the = may I prosper]
There was never yeoman in merry England
I longed so sore to see.

"Where is the monk that these should have brought?"
Our king can say.
"By my troth," said Little John,
"He died after the way."

The king gave Much and Little John
Twenty pound in certain,
And made them yeomen of the crown,
And bade them go again.

He gave John the seal in hand,
The sheriff for to bear,
To bring Robin him to,
And no man do him dere.   [dere = harm]

John took his leave at our king,
The sooth as I you say;   [sooth = truth]
The next way to Nottingham
To take he yede the way.   [yede = went]

When John came to Nottingham
The gates were sparred ychon;   [sparred ychon = all barred]
John called up the porter,
He answered soon anon.   [anon = soon]

"What is the cause," said Little John,
"Thou sparrst the gates so fast?"
"Because of Robin Hood," said porter,
"In deep prison is cast.

"John and Much and Will Scathlok,
For sooth as I you say,
They slew our men upon our walls,
And sawten us every day."   [sawten = assault]

Little John spyrred after the sheriff,   [spyrred = asked]
And soon he him found;
He opened the king's privy seal,
And gave him in his hand.

When the sheriff saw the king's seal,
He did off his hood anon: [anon = soon]
"Where is the monk that bear the letters?"
He said to Little John.

"He is so fain of him," said Little John,   [fain = glad]
"Forsooth as I you say,
He has made him abbot of Westminster,
A lord of that abbey."

The sheriff made John good cheer,
And gave him wine of the best;
At night they went to their bed,
And every man to his rest.

When the sheriff was on sleep,
Drunken of wine and ale,
Little John and Much forsooth

Took the way unto the jail.

Little John called up the jailer,
And bade him rise anon;   [anon = soon]
He said Robin Hood had broken the prison,
And out of it was gone.

The porter rose anon certain,
As soon as he heard John call;
Little John was ready with a sword,
And bare him through to the wall.   [bare = stabbed]

"Now will I be jailer," said Little John,
And took the keys in hand;
He took the way to Robin Hood,
And soon he him unbound.

He gave him a good sword in his hand,
His head therewith to keep,
And there as the walls were lowest
Anon down can they leap.

Be that the cock began to crow,
The day began to spring;
The sheriff found the jailer dead,
The common bell made he ring.

He made a cry throughout all the town,
Whether he be yeoman or knave,
That cowthe bring him Robin Hood,   [cowthe = could]
His warison he should have.   [warison = reward]

"For I dare never," said the sheriff,
"Come before our king;
For if I do, I wot certain   [wot = know]
Forsooth he will me hang."

The sheriff made to seek Nottingham,   [seek = search]

Both by street and sty,
And Robin was in merry Sherwood,
As light as leaf on lynde. [lynde = linden tree]

Then bespake good Little John,
To Robin Hood can he say,
"I have done thee a good turn for an ill,
Quit me when thou may.

"I have done thee a good turn," said Little John,
"Forsooth as I thee say;
I have brought thee under the greenwood lyne;   [lyne = linden tree]
Farewell, and have good day."

"Nay, by my troth," said Robin,
"So shall it never be;
I make thee master," said Robin,
"Of all my men and me."

"Nay, by my troth," said Little John,
"So shall it never be;
But let me be a fellow," said Little John,
"No noder kepe I be."   [No other I want to be]

Thus John got Robin Hood out of prison,
Certain without lie;
When his men saw him whole and sound,
Forsooth they were full fain.   [fain = glad]

They filled in wine and made them glad,
Under the leaves small,
And ate pasties of venison,
That good was with ale.

Than word came to our king
How Robin Hood was gone,
And how the sheriff of Nottingham
Durst never look him upon.

Then bespake our comely king,
In an anger high:
"Little John has beguiled the sheriff,
In faith so has he me.

"Little John has beguiled us both,
And that full well I see;
Or else the sheriff of Nottingham
High hanged should he be.

"I made him yeomen of the crown,
And gave him fee with my hand;
I gave him grith," said our king,   [grith = pardon]
"Throughout all merry England.

"I gave him grith," then said our king;
"I say, so mot I the,   [mot I the = may I prosper]
Forsooth such a yeoman as he is one
In all England are not three.

"He is true to his master," said our king;
"I say, by sweet Saint John,
He loves better Robin Hood
Than he does us ychon.   [ychon = each one]

"Robin Hood is ever bound to him,
Both in street and stall;
Speke no more of this matter," said our king,
"But John has beguiled us all."

Thus ends the talking of the monk
And Robin Hood I wis;   [wis = know]
God, that is ever a crowned king,
Bring us all to His bliss!

Robin Hood and the Potter

Like "Robin Hood and the Monk," this ballad begins with Robin Hood losing a bet to Little John. As Little John predicted, the potter fights with and beats Robin, though he just has a staff against Robin's sword. As in many other ballads, the fight with a potter leads to friendship.

This ballad also has the familiar theme of tricking the sheriff, with Robin Hood as the successful trickster. Robin takes the potter's goods to Nottingham, sells them at a low price, wins an archery contest, and convinces the sheriff to come to the forest with him to capture Robin Hood. When they get to the forest, he calls his men and takes the sheriff's horse and the goods he brought with him, giving the sheriff a palfrey to take back to his wife, who laughs at the sheriff when he gets home.

It seems unlikely that Robin Hood comes out ahead financially in this ballad. He wins 40 shillings in an archery contest and takes the sheriff's horse and goods, but he loses 40 shillings in his bet with Little John, gives the sheriff's wife a palfrey and gold ring, and gives the potter ten pounds for pots that he sold for less than their actual worth of two-thirds of a pound. The point of the ballad is that he was generous to his friends and to women, and that he swindled the sheriff to punish his enemy. Presumably, he had enough money from robbing all the people who passed through the forest that he did not have to worry about the cost of this adventure.

This ballad survives in a manuscript from about 1500 owned by Cambridge University, a collection of poems. The story was obviously well known, since part of a play about the same story also survives is included in this book.

Fitt 1   [fitt or fit = section of a poem]

In summer, when the leaves spring,
The blossoms on every bough,
So merry do the birds sing
In woods merry now.

Hearken, good yeomen,
Comely, courteous, and good,
One of the best that ever bore bow,
His name was Robin Hood.

Robin Hood was the yeoman's name,
That was both courteous and free;
For the love of our lady,
All women worshipped he.

But as the good yeoman stood on a day,
Among his merry maney,   [maney = group of men]
He was ware of a proud potter,
Came driving over the leye.   [leye = land]

"Yonder cometh a proud potter," said Robin,
"That long hath hanted this way;   [hanted = passed]
He was never so courteous a man
One penny of pavage to pay."   [pavage = toll]

"I met him but at Wentbreg," said Little John,
"And therefore evil mot he the!   [evil mot he the = may he do badly]
Such three strokes he me gave,
Yet by my sides cleave they.   [They still are splitting my sides]

I lay forty shillings," said Little John,
"To pay it this same day,
There is not a man among us all
A wed shall make him lay."   [lay a wed = make a payment]

"Here is forty shillings," said Robin,
"More, an thou dare say,   [an = if]
That I shall make that proud potter,
A wed to me shall he lay."

There this money they laid,
They took it a yeoman to keep;
Robin before the potter he breyed,   [breyed = jumped]
And bade him stand still.

Hands upon his horse he laid,
And bade the potter stand full still;
The potter shortly to him said,
"Fellow, what is thy will?"

"All these three year, and more, potter," he said,
"Thou hast hanted this way,   [hanted = passed]
Yet were thou never so courteous a man
One penny of pavage to pay."   [pavage = toll]

"What is thy name," said the potter,
"For pavage thou ask of me?"
"Robin Hood is my name,
A wed shall thou leave me."   [wed = payment]

"Wed will I non leave," said the potter,   [non = not]
"Nor pavage will I non pay;
Away thy hand from my horse!
I will thee tene else, by my fay."   [tene = harm, fay = faith]

The potter to his cart he went,
He was not to seek;   [not to seek = not hidden]
A good two-hand staff thereout he hent,   [hent = took]
Before Robin he leaped.

Robin out with a sword bent,
A buckler in his hand;   [buckler = small shield]

The potter to Robin he went,
And said, "Fellow, let my horse go."

Together then went these two yeomen,
It was a good sight to see;
Thereof low Robin his men,   [low Robin his men = Robin's men laughed]
There they stood under a tree.

Little John to his fellow he said,
"Yend potter will stiffly stand":   [yend = that, stiffly = steadfastly]
The potter, with an acward stroke,   [acward = back-handed]
Smote the buckler out of his hand.

And ere Robin might get it again
His buckler at his feet,
The potter in the neck him took,   [took = hit]
To the ground soon he yede.   [yede = went]

That saw Robin his men,   [Robin his = Robin's]
As they stood under a bough;
"Let us help our master," said Little John,
"Yonder potter," said he, "else will him slo."   [slo = slay]

These wight yeomen with a breyde,   [wight = strong, breyde = rush]
To this master they came.
Little John to his master said,
"Who hath the wager won?

"Shall I have your forty shillings," said Little John,
"Or ye, master, shall have mine?"
"If they were a hundred," said Robin,
"In faith, they been all thine."

"It is full little courtesy," said the potter,
"As I have heard wise men say,
If a poor yeoman come driving over the way,
To let him of his journey."   [let = hinder]

"By my troth, thou sayst sooth," said Robin,   [sooth = truth]
"Thou sayst good yeomanry;
An thou drive forth every day,   [an = if]
Thou shalt never be let for me."   [let for = hindered by]

"I will pray thee, good potter,
A fellowship will thou have?
Give me thy clothing, and thou shalt have mine;
I will go to Nottingham."

"I grant thereto," said the potter,
"Thou shalt find me a fellow good;
But thou can sell my pot well,
Come again as thou yede."   [yede = went]

"Nay, by my troth," said Robin,
"And then I beshrew my head,   [beshrew = curse]
If I bring any pots again,
And any wife well them chepe."   [chepe = buy]

Then spake Little John,
And all his fellows heynd,   [heynd = friendly]
"Master, be well ware of the sheriff of Nottingham,
For he is little our friend."

"Through the help of Our Lady,
Fellows, let me alone.
Heyt war howte!" said Robin,   [Heyt war howte = giddyap]
"To Nottingham will I gon."   [gon = go]

Robin went to Nottingham,
These pots for to sell;
The potter abode with Robin's men,
There he fared not evil.   [fared not evil = did well]

Though Robin drove on his way,
So merry over the land:

There is more, and after is to say,
The best is beheynde.   [beheynde = to come]

Fitt 2

When Robin came to Nottingham,
The sooth if I should say,   [sooth = truth]
He set up his horse anon,   [anon = soon]
And gave him oats and hay.

In the midst of the town,
There he showed his ware;
"Pots! pots!" he gan cry full soon,
"Have hansell for the mare!"   [hansell for the mare =
a bonus for buying more]

Full effen against the sheriff's gate   [Full effen = right]
Showed he his chaffare;   [chaffare = bargains]
Wives and widows about him drew,
And cheped fast of his ware.   [cheped = bought]

Yet "Pots, great cheap!" cried Robin,   [great = very]
"I love evil these to stand."   [love evil = hate]
And all that saw him sell
Said he had been no potter long.

The pots that were worth pence five,
He sold them for pence three;
Privily said man and wife,
"Yonder potter shall never the."   [the = thrive]

Those Robin sold full fast,
Till he had pots but five;
Up he them took off his car,
And send them to the sheriff's wife.

Thereof she was full fain,   [fain = glad]

"Gereamarsey," said she, "sir, then,   [Gereamarsey = many thanks]
When ye come to thus country again,
I shall buy of the pots, so mo I the."   [so mo I the = so may I thrive]

"Ye shall have of the best," said Robin,
And sware by the Trinity;
Full courteously she gan him call,
"Come dine with the sheriff and me."

"God have mercy," said Robin,
"Your bidding shall be done."
A maiden in the pots gan bear,
Robin and the sheriff wife followed anon.   [anon = soon]

When Robin in to the hall came,
The sheriff soon he met;
The potter cowed of courtesy,   [cowed of = understood]
And soon the sheriff he gret.   [gret = greeted]

"Lo, sir, what this potter hath give you and me,
Five pots small and great!"
"He is full welcome," said the sheriff,
"Let us wash, and to meat."

As they sat at their meat,
With a noble cheer,   [noble cheer = fine food]
Two of the sheriff's men gan speak
Of a great wager,

Of a shooting, was good and fine,   [a shooting = a shooting match]
Was made the other day,
Of forty shillings, the sooth to say,   [sooth = truth]
Who should this wager gain.

Still then sat this proud potter,
Thus than thought he,
As I am a true Christian man,
This shooting will I see.

When they had fared of the best,
With bread and ale and wine,
To the bots the made them prest,   [bots = target, prest = hurry]
With bows and bolts full fine.

The sheriff's men shot full fast,
As archers that weren prowe,   [weren prowe = were skilled]
There came non ner nigh the mark   [non ner nigh = not nearer]
By half a good archer's bow.   [by = than]

Still then stood the proud potter,
Thus then said he;
"An I had a bow, by the Rood,   [an = if, rood = cross]
One shot should you see."

"Thou shall have a bow," said the sheriff,
"The best that thou will choose of three;
Thou seemst a stalwart and a strong,
Assay shall thou be."   [assay = assayed, tested]

The sheriff commanded a yeoman that stood them by
After bows to wend;   [wend = go]
The best bow that the yeoman brought
Robin set on a string.

"Now shall I wit an thou be good,   [wit an = know if]
And pull it up to thy ear."
"So God me help," said the proud potter,
"This is but right weak gear."*

To a quequer Robin went,   [quequer = quiver]
A good bolt out he took;
So nigh on to the mark he went,
He failed not a foot.

---

* The sheriff says he will see if Robin Hood is a good archer who can draw it all
the way, to the point where his hand reaches his ear. Robin Hood replies that it
is a weak bow and easy to draw.

All they shot a bowthe again,   [a bowthe again = another round]
The sheriff's men and he;
Off the mark he would not fail,
He cleft the preke on three.   [preke on three = peg in three]

The sheriff's men thought great shame   [thought it a great shame]
The potter the mastery won;
The sheriff lowe and made good game,   [lowe = laughed]
And said, "Potter, thou art a man.
Thou art worthy to bear a bow
In what place that thou go."

"In my cart I have a bow,
Forsooth," he said, "and that a good;
In my cart is the bow
That gave me Robin Hood."

"Knowest thou Robin Hood?" said the sheriff,
"Potter, I pray thee tell thou me."
"A hundred turn I have shot with him,
Under his tortyll-tree."   [tortyll = meeting]
"I had liever nar a hundred pound," said the sheriff,   [liever nar =
And swear by the Trinity,   rather than]
"That the false outlaw stood by me."

"An ye will do after my red," said the potter,   [an = if, red = advice]
"And boldly go with me,
And to-morrow, ere we eat bread,
Robin Hood will we see."

"I will quite thee," quoth the sheriff,   [quite = requite]
"And swear by God of meythey."   [of meythey = almighty]
Shooting they left, and home they went,   [left = stopped]
Their supper was ready dight.   [dight = prepared]

Fitt 3

Upon the morrow, when it was day,
He bosked him forth to ride;   [bosked = hurried]
The potter his cart forth gan ray,   [forth gan ray = began to bring forth]
And would not leave behind.

He took leave of the sheriff's wife,
And thanked her of all thing:
"Dame, for my love an ye will this wear,   [an = if]
I give you here a gold ring."

"Gramercy," said the wife,   [gramercy = many thanks]
"Sir, God eylde it thee."   [eylde = reward]
The sheriff's heart was never so leythe,   [leythe = light]
The fair forest to see.

And when he came in to the forest,
Under the leaves green,
Birds there sang on boughs prest,   [prest = actively]
It was great joy to see.

"Here it is merry to be," said Robin,
"For a man that had aught to spend;
By my horn ye shall awet   [awet = come to know]
If Robin Hood be here."

Robin set his horn to his mouth,
And blow a blast that was full good;
That heard his men that there stood,
Far down in the wood.
"I hear my master blow," said Little John,
They ran as they were wode.   [wode = crazy]

When they to their master came,
Little John would not spare;   [spare = hold back]
"Master, how have you fare in Nottingham?
How have you sold your ware?"

"Yea, by my troth, Little John,
Look thou take no care;
I have brought the sheriff of Nottingham,
For all our chaffare."   [chaffare = bargaining]

"He is full welcome," said Little John,
"This tiding is full good."
The sheriff had liever nar a hundred pound   [liever nar = rather than]
He had never seen Robin Hood.

"Had I wist that before,   [wist = known]
At Nottingham when we were,
Thou should not come in fair forest
Of all these thousand eyre."   [eyre = years]

"That wot I well," said Robin,   [wot = know]
"I thank God that ye be here;
Therefore shall ye leave your horse with us,
And all your other gear."

"That fend I God forbid," quoth the sheriff,   [fend = hope]
"So to lose my good."
"Hither ye came on horse full high,
And home shall ye go on foot;
And greet well thy wife at home,
The woman is full good.

"I shall her send a white palfrey,
It hambellet as the wind,   [hambellet = trots]
Nere for the love of your wife,   [nere = if not]
Of more sorrow should you sing."

Thus parted Robin Hood and the sheriff;
To Nottingham he took the way;
His wife fair welcomed him home,
And to him gan she say:

"Sir, how have you fared in green forest?
Have ye brought Robin home?"
"Dame, the devil speed him, both body and bone;
I have had a full great scorn.

"Of all the good that I have lade to green wood,   [lade = brought]
He hath take it from me;
All but this fair palfrey,
That he hath send to thee."

With that she took up a loud laughing,
And sware by Him that died on tree,   [tree = cross]
"Now have you paid for all the pots
That Robin gave to me.

"Now ye be come home to Nottingham.
Ye shall have good enow."   [good enow = enough possessions]
Now speak we of Robin Hood,
And of the potter under the green bough.

"Potter, what was they pots worth
To Nottingham that I ledde with me?"   [ledde = brought]
"They were worth two nobles," said he, [noble = one-thirds of a pound]
"So mot I treyffe or the;   [mot I treyffe or the = might I prosper or thrive]
So could I had for them,
An I had be there."   [an I had be = if I had been]

"Thou shalt have ten pound," said Robin,
"Of money fair and free;
And ever when thou comest to green wood,
Welcome, potter, to me."

Thus parted Robin, the sheriff, and the potter,
Underneath the green wood tree;
God have mercy on Robin Hood's soul,
And save all good yeomanry!

Merry·Robin·stops·a·Sorrowful·Knight·

A Gest of Robin Hood, First Half

"A Gest of Robin Hood" is by far the longest of the early ballads. Scholars believe that the final composition of the Gest is later than the composition of the other early ballads, because the other ballads tell just one story, while the Gest is a more complex work, which weaves together a number of earlier stories.

It is so long that it could not have been performed all at once. The first four fitts and the second four fitts form two distinct stories, each made by weaving together several stories. To make it more readable, this book divides the Gest into these two parts.

In Fitts 1 and 2, Robin waits for some unusual guest to arrive before eating dinner, which is common in old English poetry. An impoverished knight arrives, they dine, and Robin lends the knight 400 pounds so he can pay his debt and keep his land. After going to pay his debt, the knight stops at a contest on his way back to Robin Hood.

In Fitt 3, Little John tricks the Sheriff of Nottingham into making him his servant, steals the sheriff's goods, and brings them to Robin Hood. Then he meets the sheriff in the woods and tricks him into going to see Robin Hood. Robin forces the Sheriff to swear an oath not to hurt him. This Fitt can stand alone, and it presumably was originally a separate ballad.

In Fitt 4, Robin again wants an unusual guest before eating dinner and sends men to Barnesdale to find one. They force a monk to come back with them. Robin takes the monk's 800 pounds, saying that Mary has paid him back well for the 400 pounds he loaned the knight. When the knight returns, Robin gives him the 400 pounds extra he got from the monk. The return of the knight ties the fourth fitt together with the first and second, after the unrelated story in Fitt 3.

This is the one early ballad where Robin Hood steals from the rich and gives to the poor, which he became famous for doing in subsequent versions of the legend. At first, after feeding the knight, Robin asks him to pay for his dinner—which actually means taking all the money his guest has, as we can see when he takes all of the 800 pounds that the monk has—but after finding that the knight is so poor that he is about to lose his land, Robin lends him money instead.

He also tells his men not to rob the poor, saying:

"But look ye do no husband [farmer] harm,
That tilleth with his plough.
No more ye shall no good yeoman
That walketh by green wood shawe [grove],

Likewise, when he sends his men to find the second dinner guest, he says:

Of my goods he shall have some,
If he be a poor man

but he ends up taking the monk's goods after finding he is a rich man.

There is no manuscript version of this ballad, but it is included in two books that were printed around 1510,

Fitt 1

Lythe and listen, gentlemen,   [lythe = listen]
That be of freeborn blood;
I shall you tell of a good yeoman,
His name was Robin Hood.

Robin was a proud outlaw,
Whilst he walked on ground:
So courteous an outlaw as he was one
Was never non found.

Robin stood in Barnesdale,
And leaned him to a tree,
And by him stood Little John,

A good yeoman was he.

And also did good Scarlock,   [Scarlock = Will Scarlock or Scarlet]
And Much, the miller's son:
There was none inch of his body
But it was worth a grome.   [grome = man]

Then bespake Little John
All unto Robin Hood:
"Master, an ye would dine betime   [an = if]
It would do you much good."

Than bespake him good Robin:
"To dine have I no lust,
Till that I have some bold baron,
Or some uncouth guest.   [uncouth = unusual]

"Here shall come a lord or sire
That may pay for the best,
Or some knight or squire,
That dwelleth here by west."

A good manner then had Robin;   [manner = habit]
In land where that he were,
Every day ere he would dine
Three masses would he hear.

The one in the worship of the Father,
And another of the Holy Ghost,
The third of Our dear Lady,
That he loved allther most.   [allther = of all the]

Robin loved our dear Lady:
For doubt of deadly sin,   [doubt = fear]
Would he never do company harm
That any woman was in.

"Master," then said Little John,

"An we our board shall spread,
Tell us whither that we shall go,
And what life that we shall lead.

"Where we shall take, where we shall leave,
Where we shall abide behind;
Where we shall rob, where we shall reve,   [reve = take by force]
Where we shall beat and bind."

"Thereof no force," then said Robin;   [thereof no force = it doesn't matter]
"We shall do well enow;   [enow = enough]
But look ye do no husband harm,   [husband = farmer]
That tilleth with his plough.

"No more ye shall no good yeoman
That walketh by green wood shawe,   [shawe = grove]
Ne no knight ne no squire
That will be a good fellow.

"These bishops and these archbishops,
Ye shall them beat and bind;
The high sheriff of Nottingham,
Him hold ye in your mind."

"This word shall be hold," said Little John,
"And this lesson we shall lere;   [lere = learn]
It is fer dayes, God send us a guest,   [fer dayes = far into the day]
That we were at our dinner!"

"Take thy good bow in thy hand," said Robin;
"Let Much wend with thee: [wend = go]
And so shall William Scarlock,
And no man abide with me.

"And walk up to the Saylis,
And so to Watlinge Street,
And wait after some uncouth guest,
Up chance ye may them meet.

"Be he earl, or any baron,
Abbot, or any knight,
Bring him to lodge to me;
His dinner shall be dight."   [dight = prepared]

They went up to the Saylis,
These yeoman all three;
They looked east, they looked west;
They might no man see.

But as they looked in to Barnesdale,
By a derne street,   [derne = secret]
Then came a knight riding,
Full soon they gan him meet.

All dreary was his semblance,
And little was his pride;
His one foot in the stirrup stood,
That other waved beside.

His hood hanged in his eyen two;   [eyen = eyes]
He rode in simple array,   [array = clothing]
A sorrier man than he was one
Rode never in summer day.

Little John was full courteous,
And set him on his knee:
"Welcome be ye, gentle knight,
Welcome are ye to me.

"Welcome be thou to green wood,
Hende knight and free;   [hende = courteous]
My master hath abiden you fasting,   [abiden = awaited]
Sir, all these hour three."

"Who is thy master?" said the knight;
John said, "Robin Hood."
"He is good yeoman," said the knight,

"Of him I have heard much good.

"I grant," he said, "with you to wend,   [wend = go]
My brethern, all in fere;   [in fere = together]
My purpose was to have dined to day
At Blith or Dancastere."

Forth than went this gentle knight,
With a careful chere;   [careful chere = expression full of care]
The tears out of his iyen ran,   [iyen = eyes]
And fell down by his lere.   [lere = face]

They brought him to the lodge door,
When Robin him gan see,
Full courteously did off his hood   [did off = took off]
And set him on his knee.

"Welcome, sir knight," than said Robin,
"Welcome art thou to me;
I have abiden you fasting, sir,   [abiden = awaited]
All these hours three."

Than answered the gentle knight,
With words fair and free:
"God thee save, good Robin,
And all thy fair meyné."   [meyné = company]

They washed together and wiped both,
And set to their dinner;
Bread and wine they had right enough,
And noumbles of the deer.   [noumbles = organ meats or loin cuts]

Swans and pheasants they had full good,
And fowls of the river;
There failed none so little a bird
That ever was bred on bryre.   [bryre = branch]

"Do gladly, sir knight," said Robin;

"Gramercy, sir," said he,   [gramercy = many thanks]
"Such a dinner had I not
Of all these weeks three.

 "If I come again, Robin,
Here by this country,
As good a dinner I shall thee make
As that thou hast made to me."

"Gramercy, knight," said Robin,   [gramercy = many thanks]
"My dinner when that I it have;
I was never so greedy, by dear worthy God,   [greedy = hungry]
My dinner for to crave.

"But pay ere ye wend," said Robin;   [wend = go]
"Me thinketh it is good right;
It was never the manner, by dear worthy God,   [manner = usage]
A yeoman to pay for a knight."

"I have nought in my coffers," said the knight,
"That I may proffer for shame."
" Little John, go look," said Robin,
"Ne let not for no blame."   [Do not delay because someone
                                              might say it is wrong]

"Tell me truth," then said Robin,
"So God have part of thee."   [have part = protect]
"I have no more but ten shillings," said the knight,
"So God have part of me."

"If thou hast no more," said Robin,
"I will not one penny,
And if thou have need of any more,
More shall I lend thee.

"Go now forth, Little John,
The truth tell thou me:
If there be no more but ten shillings,
No penny that I see."   [that I see = of it I take]

Little John spread down his mantle
Full fair upon the ground,
And there he found in the knight's coffer
But even half pound.   [half pound = ten shillings]

Little John let it lie full still,
And went to his master full low;
"What tidings John?" said Robin;
"Sir, the knight is true enow."   [enow = enough]

"Fill of the best wine," said Robin,
"The knight shall begin;
Much wonder thinketh me
Thy clothing is so thin.

"Tell me one word," said Robin,
"And counsel shall it be:
I trowe thou wert made a knight of force,   [trowe = think]
Or else of yeomanry.

"Or else thou hast been a sorry husband,
And lived in stroke and strife,   [stroke = conflict]
An okerer or else a lecher," said Robin,   [okerer = usurer]
"With wrong hast led thy life."

"I am none of those," said the knight,
"By God that made me;
An hundred winter here before
Mine ancestors knights have be.

"But oft it hath befall, Robin,
A man hath be disgraced,
But God that sitteth in heaven above
May amend his state.

"Within this two year, Robin," he said,
"My neighbors well it weened,   [weened = knew]
Four hundred pound of good money
Full well then might I spend.

"Now have I no good," said the knight,
"God hath shaped such an end,
But my children and my wife,
Till God it may amend."

"In what manner," than said Robin,
"Hast thou lorne thy richesse?"   [lorne = lost]
"For my great folly," he said,
"And for my kindness.

"I had a son, forsooth, Robin,
That should have been mine heir,
When he was twenty winter old,
In field would joust full fair.

"He slew a knight of Lancaster,
And a squire bold;
For to save him in his right
My goods beth set and sold.   [beth = are]

"My lands beth set to wedde, Robin,   [wedde = security for a loan]
Until a certain day,
To a rich abbot here beside
Of Saint Mary Abbey."

"What is the sum?" said Robin;
"Truth then tell thou me."
"Sir," he said, "four hundred pound;
The abbot told it to me."   [told = counted]

"Now an thou lose thy land," said Robin,   [an = if]
"What will fall of thee?"
"Hastily I will me buske," said the knight,   [buske = hurry]
"Over the salt sea,

"And see where Christ was quick and dead,   [quick = alive]
On the mount of Calvary;
Fare well, friend, and have good day;
It may no better be."

Tears fell out of his iyen two;   [iyen = eyes]
He would have gone his way.
"Farewell, friend, and have good day;
I ne have no more to pay."

"Where be thy friends?" said Robin.
"Sir, never one will me know:
While I was rich enow at home   [enow = enough]
Great boast then would they blow.

"And now they run away from me,
As beasts in a row;
They take no more heed of me
Than they had me never saw."

For ruth then wept Little John,   [ruth = pity]
Scarlok and Much in fere;   [in fere = together]
"Fill of the best wine," said Robin,
"For here is a simple cheer.

"Hast thou any friend," said Robin,
"Thy borrow that would be?"   [thy borrow would be =
"I have none," then said the knight,   would guarantee the loan]
"But God that died on tree."   [tree = cross]

"Do away thy japes," then said Robin,   [japes = jokes]
"Thereof will I right none;
Weenest thou I would have God to borrow,   [ween = think]
Peter, Paul, or John?

"Nay, by Him that me made,
And shope both sun and moon,   [shope = shaped]
Find me a better borrow," said Robin,
"Or money getst thou none."

"I have none other," said the knight,
"The sooth for to say,   [sooth = truth]
But if it be our dear Lady;

She failed me never ere this day."

"By dear worthy God," said Robin,
"To search all England through,
Yet found I never to my pay
A much better borrow.

"Come now fourth, Little John.
And go to my treasury,
And bring me four hundred pound,
And look well told it be."   [told = counted]

Fourth then went Little John,
And Scarlock went before;
He told out four hundred pounde
By eighteen and two score.

"Is this well told?" said little Much;
John said, "What grieveth thee?
It is alms to help a gentle knight,
That is fall in poverty.   [fall = fallen]

"Master," then said Little John,
"His clothing is full thin;
Ye must give the knight a livery,
To lappe his body therein.   [lappe = wrap]

"For ye have scarlet and green, master,
And many a rich array;
There is no merchant in merry England
So rich, I dare well say."

"Take him three yards of every color,
And look well meet that it be."   [meet = befitting]
Little John took none other measure
But his bow-tree.   [bow-tree = the wooden part of the bow]

And at every handful that he met

He leped foots three.   [leped = added]
"What devil's draper," said little Much,   [draper = cloth merchant]
"Thinkst thou for to be?"

Scarlock stood full still and laugh,
And said, "By God Almight,
John may give him good measure,
For it costeth him but light."

"Master," then said Little John
To gentle Robin Hood,
"Ye must give the knight a horse,
To lede home this good."   [lede = carry]

"Take him a gray courser," said Robin,
"And a saddle new;
He is Our Lady's messenger;
God grant that he be true."

"And a good palfrey," said little Much,
"To maintain him in his right."
"And a pair of boots," said Scarlock,
"For he is a gentle knight."

"What shalt thou give him, Little John?" said Robin;
"Sir, a pair of gilt spurs clean,
To pray, for all this company,
God bring him out of tene."   [tene = harm]

"When shall my day be," said the knight,   [day = date to repay]
"Sir, an your will be?"   [an = if]
"This day twelve month," said Robin,
"Under this green-wood tree.

"It were great shame," said Robin,
"A knight alone to ride,
Without squire, yeoman, or page,
To walk by his side.

"I shall thee lend Little John, my man,
For he shall be thy knave;
In a yeoman's stead he may thee stand,
If thou great need have."

Fitt 2

Now is the knight gone on his way:
This game him thought full good;
When he looked on Barnesdale
He blessed Robin Hood.

And when he thought on Barnesdale,
On Scarlock, Much, and John,
He blessed them for the best company
That ever he in come.   [in come = came into]

Then spake that gentle knight,
To Little John gan he say,
"To-morrow I must to York town,
To Saint Mary abbey.

"And to the abbot of that place
Four hundred pound I must pay;
And but I be there upon this night   [but = unless]
My land is lost for ay."   [for ay = for ever]

The abbot said to his convent,
There he stood on ground,
"This day twelve month came there a knight
And borrowed four hundred pound.

"He borrowed four hundred pound,
Upon all his land free;
But he come this ilke day   [but = unless, ilke = same]
Disherit shall he be."   [he will lose his inherited land]

"It is full early," said the prior,
"The day is not yet far gone;
I had liever to pay an hundred pound,   [liever = rather]
And lay down anon.   [anon = soon]

"The knight is far beyond the sea,
In England right,   [defending England's rights]
And suffreth hunger and cold,
And many a sorry night.

"It were great pity," said the prior,
"So to have his land;
An ye be so light of your conscience,   [an = if]
Ye do to him much wrong."

"Thou art ever in my beard," said the abbot,
"By God and Saint Richard."
With that came in a fat-headed monk,
The high cellarer.   [cellarer = monk who manages food and drink]

"He is dead or hanged," said the monk,
"By God that bought me dear,
And we shall have to spend in this place
Four hundred pound by year."

The abbot and the high cellarer
Start forth full bold,
The high justice of England
The abbot there did hold.

The high justice and many mo
Had take in to their hand
Wholly all the knight's debt,
To put that knight to wrong.

They deemed the knight wonder sore,   [deemed = judged, sore = harshly]
The abbot and his meyné: [meyné = company]
"But he come this ilke day   [but = unless, ilke = same]

Disherit shall he be."   [he will lose his inherited land]

"He will not come yet," said the justice,
"I dare well undertake."
But in sorrow time for them all   [sorrow = sorrowful]
The knight came to the gate.

Then bespake that gentle knight
Until his meyné: [until = unto, meyné = company]
"Now put on your simple weeds   [weeds = clothing]
That ye brought from the sea."

They put on their simple weeds,
They came to the gates anon;   [anon = soon]
The porter was ready himself,
And welcomed them every one.

"Welcome, sir knight," said the porter;
"My lord to meat is he,   [to meat = eating]
And so is many a gentle man,
For the love of thee."

The porter swore a full great oath,
"By God that made me,
Here be the best coressed horse   [coressed = bodied]
That ever yet saw I me.

"Lead them in to the stable," he said,
"That eased might they be."
"They shall not come therein," said the knight,
"By God that died on a tree."   [tree = cross]

Lords were to meat ysette   [ysette = seated]
In that abbot' hall;
The knight went forth and kneeled down,
And salued them great and small.   [salued = greeted]

"Do gladly, sir abbot," said the knight,

"I am come to hold my day."
The first word the abbot spake,
"Hast thou brought my pay?"

"Not one penny," said the knight,
"By God that maked me."
"Thou art a shrewed debtor" said the abbot;   [shrewed = cursed]
"Sir justice, drink to me.

"What dost thou here," said the abbot,
"But thou hadst brought thy pay?"   [But thou hadst = if you have not]
"For God," than said the knight,
"To pray of a longer day."   [a longer day = a longer time to pay]

"Thy day is broke," said the justice,   [thy day is broke = your day has come]
"Land getest thou none."
"Now, good sir justice, be my friend,
And fend me of my fone!"   [fend = defend, fone = foes]

"I am hold with the abbot," said the justice,
"Both with cloth and fee."*
"Now, good sir sheriff, be my friend!"
"Nay, for God," said he.

"Now, good sir abbot, be my friend,
For thy courtesy,
And hold my lands in thy hand
Till I have made the gree!   [gree = repayment]

"And I will be thy true servant,
And truly serve thee,
Till ye have four hundred pound
Of money good and free."

The abbot sware a full great oath,
"By God that died on a tree,   [tree = cross]

---

* The abbot had paid the king's justice to help press his case against the knight.
  Cloth and fee means he had paid with both money and gifts of clothing.

Get the land where thou may,
For thou getest none of me."

"By dear worthy God," then said the knight,
"That all this world wrought,
But I have my land again,   [but = unless]
Full dear it shall be bought.

"God, that was of a maiden born,
Leave us well to speed!   [let us do well]
For it is good to assay a friend   [assay = test]
Ere that a man have need."

The abbot loathly on him gan look,   [loathly = loathingly]
And villainously him gan call:
"Out," he said, "thou false knight,
Speed thee out of my hall!"

"Thou liest," then said the gentle knight,
"Abbot, in thy hall;
False knight was I never,
By God that made us all."

Up then stood that gentle knight,
To the abbot said he,
"To suffer a knight to kneel so long,
Thou canst no courtesy.

"In jousts and in tournament
Full ferre then have I be,   [ferre = in danger]
And put my self as ferre in press
As any that ever I see."

"What will ye give more," said the justice,
"An the knight shall make a release?*   [an = if]

---

* The justice wants the abbot to pay the knight so the knight will give his land to
  him, rather than just taking it for the debt and making the knight hostile to him
  permanently.

An else dare I safely swear   [an else = otherwise (without a release)]
Ye hold never your land in peace."

"An hundred pound," said the abbot;
The justice said, "Give him two."
"Nay, by God," said the knight,
"Yet get ye it not so."

"Though ye would give a thousand more,
Yet were ye never the near;   [never the near = no nearer to making a deal]
Shall there never be mine heir
Abbot, justice, ne frere."   [frere = monk]

He stert him to a board anon,   [stert= started, board = table, anon = soon]
Till a table round,
And there shook out of a bag
Even four hundred pound.

"Have here this gold, sir abbot," said the knight,
"Which that thou lentest me;
Had thou been courteous at my coming,
Rewarded shouldst thou have be."

The abbot sat still, and ate no more,
For all his royal fare;
He cast his head on his shoulder,
And fast began to stare.   [fast = fixedly]

"Take me my gold again," said the abbot,
"Sir justice, that I took thee."*
"Not a penny," said the justice,
"By God that died on tree."   [tree = cross]

"Sir abbot and ye men of law,
Now have I hold my day;
Now shall I have my land again,
For aught that you can say."

---

* The abbot wants the justice to return the fee that he paid to retain him.

The knight stert out of the door,　　　　　　[stert = started]
Away was all his care,
And on he put his good clothing,
The other he left there.

He went him forth full merry singing,
As men have told in tale;
His lady met him at the gate,
At home in Verysdale.

"Welcome, my lord," said his lady;
"Sir, lost is all your good?"
"Be merry, dame," said the knight,
"And pray for Robin Hood,

"That ever his soul be in bliss:
He holp me out of tene;　　　　　　[holp = helped, tene = harm]
Ne had be his kindness,　　　[Ne had be = if it had not been for]
Beggars had we been.

"The abbot and I accorded been,
He is served of his pay;
The god yeoman lent it me,
As I came by the way."

This knight then dwelled fair at home,
The sooth for to say.　　　　　　　　[sooth = truth]
Till he had get four hundred pound,
All ready for to pay.

He purveyed him an hundred bows,
The strings well ydight,　　　　　　[ydight = prepared]
An hundred sheaves of arrows good,
The heads burnished full bright;

And every arrow an el long,
With peacock well ydight,
Inocked all with white silver;　　[inocked = grooved where the string fits]
It was a seemly sight.

He purveyed him an hundred men,
Well harnessed in that stead.
And him self in that same sat,
And clothed in white and red.

He bare a lancegay in his hand,   [lancegay = small lance]
And a man ledde his male,   [ledde his male = carried his trunk]
And reden with a light song   [reden = rode]
Unto Barnsedale.

But at Wentbridge there was a wrestling, [wrestling = wrestling contest]
And there tarried was he,
And there was all the best yeomen
Of all the west country.

A full fair game there was up set,
A white bull up ipight,   [ipight = placed]
A great courser, with saddle and bridle,
With gold burnished full bright.

A pair of gloves, a red gold ring,
A pipe of wine, in fay;   [fay = faith]
What man that beareth him best ywis   [ywis = indeed]
The prize shall bear away.

There was a yeoman in that place,
And best worthy was he,
And for he was far and frembde bested,   [far and frembde bested =
Slain he should have be.   far from home and a
                                                  stranger who was defeated]

The knight had ruth of this yeoman,   [ruth = pity]
In place where he stood;
He said that yeoman should have no harm,
For love of Robin Hood.

The knight pressed in to the place,
An hundred followed him in fere,   [in fere = together]
With bows bent and arrows sharp,

For to shend that company.   [shend = destroy]

They shouldered all and made him room, [shouldered = stood side by side]
To wit what he would say;   [wit = know]
He took the yeoman by the hand,
And gave him all the play.   [gave him the play = made him the winner]

He gave him five mark for his wine,
There it lay on the mold,   [mold = ground]
And bade it should be set a broche,   [set a broche = opened]
Drink who so would.

Thus long tarried this gentle knight,
Till that play was done;
So long abode Robin fasting,
Three hours after the noon.

Fitt 3

Lythe and listen, gentlemen,
All that now be here,
Of Little John, that was the knight's man,
Good mirth ye shall hear.

It was upon a merry day
That young men would go shoot,
Little John fet his bow anon,   [fet = fetched, anon = soon]
And said he would them meet.

Three times Little John shot about,
And alway he slit the wand:*
The proud sheriff of Nottingham
By the marks can stand.   [stood by the targets]

* Little John split (shot right through) the wand, the most challenging archery
  contest..

The sheriff swore a full great oath:
"By Him that died on a tree,   [tree = cross]
This man is the best archer
That ever yet saw I me.

"Say me now, wight young man,   [wight = strong]
What is now thy name?
In what country were thou born,
And where is thy woning wane?"   [woning wane = dwelling place]

"In Holderness, sir, I was born,
Ywis all of my dame;   [ywis = indeed]
Men call me Reynold Greenleaf
When I am at home."

"Say me, Reynold Greenleaf,
Would thou dwell with me?
And every year I will thee give
Twenty mark to thy fee."

"I have a master," said Little John,
"A courteous knight is he;
May ye leave get of him,
The better may it be."

The sheriff got Little John
Twelve months of the knight;
Therefore he gave him right anon   [anon = soon]
A good horse and a wight.   [wight = strong]

Now is Little John the sheriff's man
God lend us well to speed!
But alway thought Little John
To quite him well his mede. [quite = requite, his mede = what he deserves]

"Now so God me help," said Little John,
"And by my true leuty,   [leuty = loyalty]
I shall be the worst servant to him

That ever yet had he."

It fell upon a Wednesday
The sheriff on hunting was gone,
And Little John lay in his bed,
And was foriete at home. [foriete = forgotten]

Therefore he was fasting
Till it was past the noon.
"Good sir steward, I pray to thee,
Give me my dinner," said Little John.

"It is long for Greenleaf
Fasting thus for to be;
Therefore I pray thee, sir steward,
My dinner give thou me."

"Shalt thou never eat ne drink," said the steward,
"Till my lord be come to town."
"I make mine avow to God," said Little John,
"I had leiver to crack thy crown." [leiver = rather]

The butler* was full uncourteous,
There he stood on floor;
He start to the buttery [buttery = where food and drink were stored]
And shut fast the door.

Little John gave the butler such a tap
His back were near in two;
Though he lived an hundred year,
The worse should he go. [he would walk worse all his life]

He sporned the door with his foot, [sporned = kicked]
It went open well and fine,
And there he made large liveray, [made large liveray = took a large amount]
Both of ale and of wine.

* The butler is the same as the steward.

"Sith ye will not dine," said Little John,   [sith = since]
"I shall give you to drink,
And though ye live an hundred winter,
On Little John ye shall think."

Little John ate, and Little John drank,
The while that he would;
The sheriff had in his kitchen a cook,
A stout man and a bold.

"I make mine avow to God," said the cook,
"Thou art a shrewed hinde   [shrewed hinde = cursed servant]
In any house for to dwell,
For to ask thus to dine."

And there he lent Little John
Good strokes three;
"I make mine avow to God," said Little John,
"These strokes liked well me.

"Thou art a bold man and hardy,
And so thinketh me;
And ere I pass from this place
Assayed better shalt thou be."   [assayed = tested]

Little John drew a full good sword,
The cook took another in hand;
They thought nothing for to flee,
But stiffly for to stand.   [stiffly = steadfastly]

There they fought sore together
Two mile way and well more;
Might neither other harm done,
The maintenance of an hour.   [maintenance = length]

"I make mine avow to God," said Little John,
"And by my true lewté,   [lewté = loyalty]
Thou art one of the best swordmen
That ever yet saw I me.

"Couldst thou shoot as well in a bow,
To green wood thou shouldst with me,
And two times in the year thy clothing
Changed should be,

"And every year of Robin Hood
Twenty mark to thy fee."
"Put up thy sword," said the cook,
"And fellows will we be."

Than he fet to Little John,   [fet = fetched]
The noumbles of a doe,   [noumbles = organ or loin meat]
Good bread, and full good wine;
They ate and drank thereto.

And when they had drunken well,
Their troths together they plight,
That they would be with Robin
That ilke same night.   [ilke = same]

They did them to the treasure house,
As fast as they might gone;
The locks, that were of full good steel,
They brake them everyone.

They took away the silver vessel,
And all that they might get;
Pecis, masars, ne spoons,   [dishes, drinking bowls, nor spoons]
Would they not forget.

Also they took the good pence,
Three hundred pound and more,
And did them straight to Robin Hood,
Under the green wood hoar.   [hoar = aged]

"God thee save, my dear master,
And Christ thee save and see!"
And then said Robin to Little John,

"Welcome might thou be."

"Also be that fair yeoman
Thou bringest there with thee;
What tidings from Nottingham?
Little John, tell thou me."

"Well thee greeteth the proud sheriff,
And send thee hear by me
His cook and his silver vessel,
And three hundred pound and three."

"I make mine avow to God," said Robin,
"And to the Trinity,
It was never by his good will
This good is come to me."

Little John there him bethought
On a shrewd wile;   [wile = trick]
Five mile in the forest he ran;
Him happed all his will.   [all he wanted happened to him]

Then he met the proud sheriff,
Hunting with hounds and horn;
Little John coude of courtesy,   [coude of = understood]
And kneeled him beforne.

"God thee save, my dear master,
And Christ thee save and see!"
"Reynold Greenleaf," said the sheriff,
"Where hast thou now be?"

"I have be in this forest;
A fair sight can I see;
It was one of the fairest sights
That ever yet saw I me.

"Yonder I saw a right fair hart,

His color is of green;
Seven score of deer upon a herd*
Be with him all bydene.   [bydene = together]

"Their tines are so sharp, master,
Of sixty, and well mo,   [mo = more]
That I durst not shot for dread,
Lest they would me slo."   [slo = slay]

"I make mine avow to God," said the sheriff,
"That sight would I fain see."
"Buske you thitherward, my dear master,   [buske = hurry]
Anon, and wend with me."   [anon = soon, wend = go]

The sheriff rode, and Little John
Of foot he was full smart,
And when they came before Robin,
"Lo, sir, here is the master-hart."

Still stood the proud sheriff,
A sorry man was he;
"Woe thee worth, Reynold Greenleaf,
Thou hast betrayed now me."

"I make mine avow to God," said Little John,
"Master, ye be to blame;
I was misserved of my dinner
When I was with you at home."

Soon he was to supper set,
And served well with silver white,
And when the sheriff saw his vessel,
For sorrow he might not eat.

"Make glad cheer," said Robin Hood,
"Sheriff, for charity,

* Robin Hood and his seven score men.

And for the love of Little John
Thy life I grant to thee."

When they had supped well,
The day was all gone;
Robin commanded Little John
To draw off his hosen and his shoon,   [his hosen and his shoon =
                                          the sheriff's tights and shoes]

His kirtell, and his coat of pie, [kirtle = tunic, pie = of two or more colors]
That was furred well and fine,
And took him a green mantel,
To lap his body therein.

Robin commanded his wight young men,   [wight = strong]
Under the green wood tree,
They should lie in that same suit,
That the sheriff might them see.

All night lay the proud sheriff
In his breach and in his shirt;   [breach = breeches]
No wonder it was, in green wood,
Though his sides gan to smart.

"Make glad cheer," said Robin Hood,
"Sheriff, for charity,
For this is our order ywis,   [ywis = indeed]
Under the green wood tree."

"This is harder order," said the sheriff,
"Than any anchor or frere; [anchor or frere = novice or friar in a monastery]
For all the gold in merry England
I would not long dwell here."

"All this twelve months," said Robin,
"Thou shalt dwell with me;
I shall thee teach, proud sheriff,
An outlaw for to be."

"Ere I be here another night," said the sheriff,
"Robin, now pray I thee,
Smite off mine head rather to-morrow,
And I forgive it thee.

"Let me go," then said the sheriff,
"For saint charity,   [saint = holy]
And I will be thy best friend
That ever yet had ye."

"Thou shalt swear me an oath," said Robin,
"On my bright brand: [brand = sword]
Shalt thou never await me scathe,   [scathe = harm]
By water ne by land."

"And if thou find any of my men,
By night or day,
Upon thine oath thou shalt swear
To help them that thou may."

Now hath the sheriff sworn his oath,
And home he began to gone;
He was as full of green wood
As ever was heap of stone.

Fitt 4

The sheriff dwelled in Nottingham
He was fain he was agone,   [was fain = wished]
And Robin and his merry men
Went to wood anon.   [anon = soon]

"Go we to dinner," said Little John,
Robin Hood said, "Nay,
For I dread Our Lady be wroth with me,
For she sent me not my pay."

"Have no doubt, master," said Little John,
"Yet is not the sun at rest;
For I dare say, and safely swear,
The knight is true and trust."

"Take thy bow in thy hand," said Robin,
"Let Much wend with thee,   [wend = go]
And so shall William Scarlock,
And no man abide with me.

"And walk up under the Sayles,
And to Watlynge-street,
And wait after such uncouth guest;   [uncouth = unusual]
Up-chance ye may them meet.

"Whether he be messenger,
Or a man that mirth's can,   [mirths can = can provide entertainment]
Of my goods he shall have some,
If he be a poor man."

Forth then stert Little John,   [stert = started]
Half in tray and tene,   [tray and tene = anger and harm]
And gird him with a full good sword,
Under a mantle of green.

They went up to the Sayles,
These yeomen all three;
They looked east, they looked west,
They might no man see.

But as they looked in Barnesdale,
By the high way,
Than were they ware of two black monks,
Each on a good palfrey.

Then bespake Little John,
To Much he gan say,
"I dare lay my life to wedde,   [wedde = wager]

The monks have brought our pay.

"Make glad cheer," said Little John,
"And dress our bows of yew,
And look your hearts be seker and sad,   [seker and sad =
Your strings trusty and true.   secure and steadfast]

"The monk hath two and fifty men
And seven somers full strong;   [somers = pack horses]
There rideth no bishop in this land
So royally, I understand.

"Brethern," said Little John,
"Here are no more but we three;
But we bring them to dinner,   [but = unless]
Our master dare we not see.

"Bend your bows," said Little John,
"Make all yon press to stand;   [press = crowd]
The foremost monk, his life and his death,
Is closed in my hand.

"Abide, churl monk," said Little John,
"No further that thou gone;
If thou dost, by dear worthy God,
Thy death is in my hand.

"And evil thrift on thy head," said Little John,   [thrift = fortune]
"Right under thy hat's band,
For thou hast made our master wroth,
He is fasting so long."

"Who is your master?" said the monk;
Little John said, "Robin Hood."
"He is a strong thief," said the monk,
"Of him heard I never good."

"Thou liest," then said Little John,

"And that shall rue thee;
He is a yeoman of the forest,
To dine he hath bode thee."   [bode = bidden]

Much was ready with a bolt,
Readily and anon;   [anon = soon]
He set the monk to-fore the breast,   [set to-fore = aimed at]
To the ground that he can gone.   [so he had to dismount]

Of two and fifty wight young yeomen   [wight = strong]
There abode not one,   [abode = stayed]
Save a little page and a groom,
To lead the somers with Little John.   [somers = pack horses]

They brought the monk to the lodge door,
Whether he were loath or leave,   [loath or leave = unwilling or willing]
For to speak with Robin Hood,
Maugré in their tethe.   [despite them]

Robin did adown his hood,   [did adown his hood =
The monk when that he see;   took down his hood, a polite gesture]
The monk was not so courteous,
His hood then let he be.

"He is a churl, master, by dear worthy God,"
Then said Little John.
"Thereof no force," said Robin,   [thereof no force = it doesn't matter]
"For courtesy can he none.

"How many men," said Robin,
"Had this monk, John?"
"Fifty and two when that we met,
But many of them be gone."

"Let blow a horn," said Robin,
"That fellowship may us know."   [fellowship = all of Robin's men]
Seven score of wight yeomen   [wight = strong]
Came prycking in a row.   [prycking = hurrying]

And everych of them a good mantle   [everych = everyone]
Of scarlet and of ray,
All they came to good Robin,
To wit what he would say.   [wit = know]

They made the monk to wash and wipe,
And sit at his dinner,
Robin Hood and Little John
They served him both in fere.   [in fere = together]

"Do gladly, monk," said Robin.
"Gramercy, sir," said he.   [gramercy = many thanks]
"Where is your abbey, when ye are at home,
And who is your avowé?"

"Saint Mary abbey," said the monk,
"Though I be simple here."   [be simple here = hold a humble office there]
"In what office?" said Robin,
"Sir, the high cellarer."   [cellarer = monk who manages food and drink]

"Ye be the more welcome," said Robin,
"So ever mote I the.   [mote I the = may I thrive]
Fill of the best wine," said Robin,
"This monk shall drink to me.

"But I have great marvel," said Robin,
"Of all this long day,
I dread Our Lady be wroth with me,
She sent me not my pay."

"Have no doubt, master," said Little John,
"Ye have no need, I say;
This monk it hath brought, I dare well swear,
For he is of her abbey."

"And she was a borrow," said Robin,
"Between a knight and me,
Of a little money that I him lent,

Under the green wood tree.

"And if thou hast that silver i-brought,
I pray thee let me see,
And I shall help thee eftsoons,   [eftsoons = in return]
If thou have need to me."

The monk swore a full great oath,
With a sorry cheer,   [cheer = expression]
"Of the borrowhood thou speakest to me,
Heard I never ere."   [ere = before]

"I make mine avow to God," said Robin,
"Monk, thou art to blame,
For God is hold a righteous man,
And so is His dame.

"Thou toldst with thine own tongue,
Thou may not say nay,
How thou art her servant,
And servest her every day.

"And thou art made her messenger,
My money for to pay;
Therfore I can the more thank
Thou art come at thy day.   [day = time the debt is due]

"What is in your coffers?" said Robin,
"True then tell thou me."
"Sir," he said, "twenty mark,
Al so mote I the."   [mote I the = may I thrive]

"If there be no more," said Robin,
"I will not one penny;
If thou hast myster of any more,   [myster = need]
Sir, more I shall lend to thee.

"And if I find more," said Robin,

"Ywis thou shalt it for gone,   [ywis = indeed, for gone = forgo]
For of thy spending silver, monk,
Thereof will I right none. [I will take none of the spending money you need]

"Go now forth, Little John,
And the truth tell thou me;
If there be no more but twenty mark,
No penny that I see."

Little John spread his mantle down,
As he had done before,
And he told out of the monk's male   [told = counted, male = chest]
Eight hundred pound and more.

Little John let it lie full still,
And went to his master in haste.
"Sir," he said, "the monk is true enow,   [true enow = faithful enough (in
Out Lady hath doubled your cast."   helping Mary to pay Robin back)]

"I make mine avow to God," said Robin,
"Monk, what told I thee?
Our Lady is the truest woman
That ever yet found I me.

"By dear worthy God," said Robin,
"To search all England through,
Yet found I never to my pay
A much better borrow.

"Fill of the best wine, and do him drink," said Robin,
"And greet well thy lady hende,   [hende = courteous]
And if she have need to Robin Hood,
A friend she shall him find.

"And if she needeth any more silver,
Come thou again to me,
And, by this token she hath me sent,
She shall have such three."   [such three = three times what she needs]

The monk was going to London-ward,
There to hold great mote,   [mote = meeting]
The knight that rode so high on horse,
To bring him under foot.

"Whither be ye away?" said Robin.
"Sir, to manors in this land,
To reckon with our reves,   [reckon with our reves = deal with out bailiffs]
That have done much wrong.

"Come now forth, Little John,
And hearken to my tale;
A better yeoman I know none,
To seek a monk's male.   [seek = search, male = baggage]

"How much is in yonder other courser?" said Robin, [courser = horse]
"The sooth must we see."   [sooth = truth]
"By Our Lady," than said the monk,
"That were no courtesy,

"To bid a man to dinner,
And sith him beat and bind."   [sith = afterward]
"It is our old manner," said Robin,
"To leave but little behind."

The monk took the horse with spur,
No longer would he abide:
"Ask to drink," then said Robin,   [ask to drink = ask permission]
"Ere that ye farther ride."

"Nay, for God," then said the monk,
"Me rueth I came so near;
For better cheep I might have dined
In Blythe or in Dankestere."

"Greet well your abbot," said Robin,
"And your prior, I you pray,
And bid him send me such a monk

To dinner every day."

Now let we that monk be still,
And speak we of that knight:
Yet he came to hold his day,   [hold his day = pay his debt in time]
While that it was light.

He did him straight to Barnesdale,
Under the green wood tree,
And he found there Robin Hood,
And all the merry meyné.   [meyné = company]

The knight light down off his good palfrey;
Robin when he gan see,
So courteously he did adown his hood,   [adown = take down his
And set him on his knee.   hood, a gesture of respect]

"God thee save, Robin Hood,
And all this company."
"Welcome be thou, gentle knight,
And right welcome to me."

Then bespake him Robin Hood,
To that knight so free:
"What need driveth thee to green wood?
I pray thee, sir knight, tell me.

"And welcome be thou, gentle knight,
Why hast thou be so long?"
"For the abbot and the high justice   [for = because]
Would have had my land."

"Hast thou thy land again?" said Robin;
"Truth than tell thou me."
"Yea, for God," said the knight,
"And that thank I God and thee.

"But take not a grief, that I have be so long;

I came by a wrestling,
And there I holp a poor yeoman,   [holp = helped]
With wrong was put behind."   [put behind = abused]

"Nay, for God," said Robin,
"Sir knight, that thank I thee;
What man that helpeth a good yeoman,
His friend then will I be."

"Have here four hundred pound," then said the knight,
"The which ye lent to me,
And here is also twenty mark
For your courtesy."

"Nay, for God," then said Robin,
"Thou broke it well for ay,   [broke = enjoy, for ay = for ever]
For Our Lady, by her cellarer,
Hath sent to me my pay.

"And if I took it i-twice,
A shame it were to me,
But truly, gentle knight,
Welcome art thou to me."

When Robin had told his tale,
He laugh and had good chere:
"By my troth," then said the knight,
"Your money is ready here."

"Broke it well," said Robin,
"Thou gentle knight so free,
And welcome be thou, gentle knight,
Under my trystell-tree.   [trystell = meeting]

"But what shall these bows do?" said Robin,
And these arrows i-feathered free?"
"By God," then said the knight,
"A poor present to thee."

"Come now forth, Little John,
And go to my treasury,
And bring me there four hundred pound;
The monk over-told it me.   [over-told = overpaid]

"Have here four hundred pound,
Thou gentle knight and true,
And buy horse and harness good,
And gild thy spurs all new.

"And if thou fail any spending,   [fail any spending =
Come to Robin Hood,   ever lack money to spend]
And by my troth thou shalt none fail,
The whiles I have any good.

"And broke well thy four hundred pound,   [broke = enjoy]
Which I lent to thee,
And make thy self no more so bare,
By the counsel of me."

Thus then holp him good Robin,   [holp = helped]
The knight all of his care:
God, that sit in heaven high,
Grant us well to fare!

The · Mighty · Fight · betwixt:
Little John · and · the · Cook:

A Gest of Robin Hood, Second Half

This ballad is the continuation of "A Gest of Robin Hood," whose first four fitts were in the previous section, but it also stands alone as a separate story.

In Fitt 5, The Sheriff of Nottingham announces an archery contest. Robin Hood goes there with seven score men and wins the contest. The sheriff tries to capture them, but they escape and take refuge in the castle of the knight whom Robin loaned money.

In Fitt 6, they defend the castle against the sheriff, who goes to London to get help from the king. Robin Hood goes back to the forest, and the sheriff captures the knight and starts back for Nottingham. Robin shoots and kills the sheriff and brings the knight back to the forest.

In Fitt 7, the king comes and seizes the knight's land. Then he disguises himself as a monk and goes to the forest, where Robin takes his 40 pounds. Later, the supposed monk hits Robin so hard as a punishment for losing at archery that they all realize that he is really the king and all kneel before him. The king invites them to come and live at court.

In Fitt 8, after living in the king's court, Robin asks a week's leave to go on a pilgrimage to a chapel of Mary Magdalene. He goes back to the forest and lives there for twenty-two years in fear of the king. Finally, he is deceived by a prioress and killed.

Notice that, the knight is named for the first time in Fitt 5:

  And there dwelled that gentle knight,
  Sir Richard at the Lee,
  That Robin had lent his good,
  Under the green wood tree.

The name is used several times in Fitts 5 to 8. It is not plausible that the author of a single work would keep a major character anonymous in the first half and then use his name in the second half. Obviously, the author of the "Gest" just put together two earlier works and modified them a bit to try to unify them by saying that the knight in both was the same person.

At the beginning of Fitt 5, the author adds a transitional stanza saying the knight left and then repeats the beginning of this separate poem.

In another example of the sort of minor modifications the author made, the sheriff took an oath not to harm Robin Hood in Fitt 4 but then begins to plot against him in Fitt 5, and the author covers the inconsistency by having Robin say that you cannot trust the sheriff. Clearly, there are two separate stories here about how Robin freed himself from the threats of the sheriff: in the first, he forces the sheriff to take an oath not to harm him, and in the second, he kills the sheriff.

The death of Robin Hood at the end obviously comes from yet another separate source, but only a brief summary is included.

Both the first and second half comprise the only early ballad where Robin Hood has his later character, robbing the rich and helping the poor.

Fitt 5

Now hath the knight his leave ytake,   [ytake = taken]
And went him on his way;
Robin Hood and his merry men
Dwelled still full many a day.

Lythe and listen, gentle men,
And hearken what I shall say,
How the proud sheriff of Nottingham
Did cry a full fair play,   [cry a play = announce a contest]

That all the best archers of the north
Should come upon a day,
And he that shooteth allther best   [allther best = best of all]
The game shall bear away.

He that shooteth allther best,
Furthest, fair and low,
At a pair of finely butts,   [finely = fine, butts = targets]
Under the green wood shawe,   [shawe = grove]

A right good arrow he shall have,
The shaft of silver white,
The head and the feathers of rich red gold,
In England is none like.

This then heard good Robin,
Under his trystell-tree: [trystell = meeting]
"Make you ready, ye wight young men;   [wight = strong]
That shooting will I see.

"Buske you, my merry young men,   [buske = hurry]
Ye shall go with me,
And I will wit the sheriff's faith,   [wit = know]
True an if he be."   [an = if]

When they had their bows ybent,
Their tackles feathered free,   [feathered free = finely feathered]
Seven score of wight young men   [wight = strong]
Stood by Robin's knee.

When they came to Nottingham,
The butts were fair and long,
Many was the bold archer
That shot with bows strong.

"There shall but six shoot with me;
The other shall keep my head,   [keep my head = watch out for me]
And stand with good bows bent,
That I be not deceived."

The fourth outlaw his bow gan bend,
And that was Robin Hood,

And that beheld the proud sheriff,
All by the butt he stood.

Thrice Robin shot a bout,
And alway he slit the wand, [slit the wand = split the stick used as the target]
And so did good Gilbert
With the White Hand.

Little John and good Scathlock
Were archers good and free;
Little Much and good Reynold,
The worst would they not be.

When they had shot a bout,
These archers fair and good,
Evermore was the best,
For sooth, Robin Hood.

Him was delivered the good arrow,
For best worthy was he;
He took the yeft so courteously,   [yeft = gift, prize]
To green wood would he.

They cried out on Robin Hood,
And great horns gan they blow:
"Woe worth thee, treason!" said Robin,
"Full evil thou art to know.

"And woe be thou! thou proud sheriff,
Thus gladding thy guest;   [gladding = making glad, meant ironically]
Other wise thou behote me   [behote = promised]
In yonder wild forest.

"But had I thee in green wood,
Under my trystell-tree,   [trystell = meeting]
Thou shouldst leave me a better wedde   [wedde = security for a loan]
Than thy true lewté   [lewté = loyalty]

Full many a bow there was bent,
And arrows let they glide;
Many a kirtle there was rent,   [kirtle = tunic]
And hurt many a side.

The outlaws' shot was so strong
That no man might them drive,
And the proud sheriff's men,
They fled away full blyve.   [blyve = quickly]

Robin saw the bushment to-broke,   [bushment = ambush]
In green wood he would have be;
Many an arrow there was shot
Among that company.

Little John was hurt full sore,
With an arrow in his knee,
That he might neither go nor ride;   [go = walk]
It was full great pity.

"Master," then said Little John,
"If ever thou lovest me,
And for that ilke Lord's love   [ilke = same]
That died upon a tree,   [tree = cross]

"And for the medes of my service,   [mede = recompense]
That I have served thee,
Let never the proud sheriff
Alive now find me.

"But take out thy brown sword,
And smite all off my head,
And give me wounds deep and wide,
No life on me be left."

"I would not that," said Robin,
"John, that thou were slaw,   [slaw = slain]
For all the gold in merry England,

Though it lay now on a raw."   [on a raw = in a row]

"God forbid," said Little Much,
"That died on a tree,   [tree = cross]
That thou shouldst, Little John,
Part our company."

Up he took him on his back,
And bare him well a mile;
Many a time he laid him down,
And shot another while.

Then was there a fair castle,
A little within the wood;
Double-ditched it was about,
And walled, by the Rood.   [Rood = Cross]

And there dwelled that gentle knight,
Sir Richard at the Lee,
That Robin had lent his good,
Under the green wood tree.

In he took good Robin,
And all his company:
"Welcome be thou, Robin Hood,
Welcome art thou to me,

"And much I thank thee of thy comfort,
And of thy courtesy,
And of thy great kindness,
Under the green wood tree.

"I love no man in all this world
So much as I do thee;
For all the proud sheriff of Nottingham,   [for all = despite]
Right here shalt thou be.

"Shut the gates, and draw the bridge,

And let no man come in,
And arm you well, and make you ready,
And to the walls ye wynne.   [wynne = go]

"For one thing, Robin, I thee behote;   [behote = promise]
I swear by Saint Quentyne,
These forty days thou wonnest with me,   [wonnest = dwell]
To sup, eat, and dine."

Boards were laid, and clothes were spread,
Readily and anon;   [anon = soon]
Robin Hood and his merry men
To meat can they gone.

Fitt 6

Lythe and listen, gentlemen,
And hearken to your song,
How the proud sheriff of Nottingham,
And men of armies strong

Full fast came to the high sheriff,
The country up to rout,
And they beset the knight's castle,
The walls all about.

The proud sheriff loud gan cry,
And said, "Thou traitor knight,
Thou keepest here the king's enemies,
Against the law and right."

"Sir, I will avow that I have done,
The deeds that here be dight,   [dight = done]
Upon all the lands that I have,
As I am a true knight.

"Wend forth, sirs, on your way,   [wend = go]

And do no more to me
Till ye wit our king's will,   [wit = know]
What he will say to thee."

The sheriff thus had his answer,
Without any lesing;   [lesing = lying]
Forth he yede to London town,   [yede = went]
All for to tell our king.

There he told him of that knight,
And eke of Robin Hood,   [eke = also]
And also of the bold archers,
That were so noble and good.

"He will avow that he hath done,   [that = what]
To maintain the outlaws strong;
He will be lord, and set you at nought,
In all the north land."

"I will be at Nottingham," said our king,
"Within this fourteenight,
And take I will Robin Hood,
And so I will that knight.

"Go now home, sheriff," said our king,
"And do as I bid thee,
And ordain good archers enow,   [enow = enough]
Of all the wide country."

The sheriff had his leave ytake,   [ytake = taken]
And went him on his way,
And Robin Hood to green wood,
Upon a certain day.

And Little John was whole of the arrow   [whole = healed]
That shot was in his knee,
And did him straight to Robin Hood,
Under the green wood tree.

Robin Hood walked in the forest,
Under the leaves green;
The proud sheriff of Nottingham
Thereof he had great tene.   [tene = harm]

The sheriff there failed of Robin Hood,
He might not have his prey;
Then he awaited this gentle knight,
Both by night and day.

Ever he waited the gentle knight,
Sir Richard at the Lee,
As he went on hawking by the river-side,
And let hawks flee.   [flee = fly]

Took he there this gentle knight,
With men of armies strong,
And led him to Nottingham ward,   [to Nottingham ward =
Bound both foot and hand.   toward Nottingham]

The sheriff sware a full great oath,
By him that died on Rood,   [rood = cross]
He had liever than an hundred pound   [liever = rather]
That he had Robin Hood.

This heard the knight's wife,
A fair lady and a free;
She set her on a good palfrey,
To green wood anon rode she.   [anon = soon]

When she came in the forest,
Under the green wood tree,
Found she there Robin Hood,
And all his fair meyné.   [meyné = company]

"God thee save, good Robin,
And all thy company;
For Our dear Lady's sake,

A boon grant thou me.

"Let never my wedded lord
Shamefully slain be;
He is fast bound to Nottingham ward,
For the love of thee."

Anon then said good Robin   [anon = soon]
To that lady so free,
"What man hath your lord take?"
"The proud sheriff," then said she.

"The sheriff hath him take," she said,
"For sooth as I thee say;
He is not yet three miles
Passed on his way."

Up than sterte good Robin,   [sterte = started]
As man that had been wode: [wode = mad, crazy]
"Buske you, my merry men,   [buske = hurry]
For him that died on Rood.   [rood = cross]

"And he that this sorrow forsaketh,
By him that died on tree,   [tree = cross]
Shall he never in green wood
No longer dwell with me."

Soon there were good bows bent,
More than seven score;
Hedge ne ditch spared they none
That was them before.

"I make mine avow to God," said Robin,
"The sheriff would I fain see,
And if I may him take,
Yquyte shall it be."   [yquyte = requited]

And when they came to Nottingham,

They walked in the street,
And with the proud sheriff ywis   [ywis = indeed]
Soon can they meet.

"Abide, thou proud sheriff," he said,
"Abide, and speak with me;
Of some tidings of our king
I would fain hear of thee.

"This seven year, by dear worthy God,
Ne yede I this fast on foot;   [yede = went]
I make mine avow to God, thou proud sheriff,
It is not for thy good."

Robin bent a full good bow,
An arrow he drove at will;
He hit so the proud sheriff
Upon the ground he lay full still.

And ere he might up arise,
On his feet to stand,
He smote of the sheriff's head
With his bright brand.   [brand = sword]

"Lie thou there, thou proud sheriff,
Evil mote thou cheve!   [evil mote thou cheve = badly may you end]
There might no man to thee trust
The whiles thou were alive."

His men drew out their bright swords,
That were so sharp and keen,
And laid on the sheriff's men,
And drived them down bydene.   [bydene = immediately]

Robin stert to that knight,   [stert = started]
And cut a-two his bond,
And took him in his hand a bow,
And bade him by him stand.

"Leave thy horse thee behind,
And learn for to run;
Thou shalt with me to green wood,
Through mire, moss, and fen.

"Thou shalt with me to green wood,
Without any leasing,   [leasing = lying]
Till that I have get us grace   [get = gotten]
Of Edward, our comely king."

Fitt 7

The king came to Nottingham,
With knights in great array,
For to take that gentle knight
And Robin Hood, and if he may.

He asked men of that country
After Robin Hood,
And after that gentle knight,
That was so bold and stout.

When they had told him the case
Our king understood their tale,
And seized in his hand
The knight's land's all.

All the compass of Lancashire
He went both far and near,
Till he came to Plomton Park;
He failed many of his deer.   [failed = lacked]

There our king was wont to see
Herds many one,
He could unneth find one deer,   [unneth = hardly]
That bare any good horn.

The king was wonder wroth withall,
And swore by the Trinity,
"I would I had Robin Hood,
With eyen I might him see.   [eyen = eyes]

"And he that would smite off the knight's head,
And bring it to me,
He shall have the knight's lands,
Sir Richard at the Lee.

"I give it him with my charter,
And seal it my hand,
To have and hold for ever more,
In all merry England."

Then bespake a fair old knight,
That was true in his fay: [fay = faith]
"Ah, my liege lord the king,
One word I shall you say.

"There is no man in this country
May have the knight's lands,
While Robin Hood may ride or go,
And bear a bow in his hands,

"That he ne shall lose his head,
That is the best ball in his hood:
Give it no man, my lord the king,
That ye will any good."

Half a year dwelled our comely king
In Nottingham, and well more;
Could he not hear of Robin Hood,
In what country that he were.

But alway went good Robin
By halk and eke by hill,   [halk = hiding place, eke = also]

And alway slew the king's deer,
And welt them at his will.   [welt = used]

Then bespake a proud forester,
That stood by our king's knee:
"If ye will see good Robin,
Ye must do after me.

"Take five of the best knights
That be in your lead,
And walk down by yon abbey,
And get you monk's weed.   [weed = clothing]

"And I will be your beadsman,
And lead you the way,
And ere ye come to Nottingham.
Mine head then dare I lay   [lay = bet]

"That ye shall meet with good Robin,
On live if that he be;   [on live = alive]
Ere ye come to Nottingham,
With eyen ye shall him see."   [eyen = eyes]

Full hastily our king was dight,   [dight = prepared]
So were his knights five,
Everych of them in monk's weed,   [everych = everyone]
And hasted them thither blyve.   [blyve = quickly]

Our king was great above his cowl,
A broad hat on his crown,
Right as he were abbot-like,
They rode up into the town.

Stiff boots our king had on,
Forsooth as I you say;
He rode singing to green wood,
The covent was clothed in gray.

His male-horse and his great somers   [male-horse = pack horse,
Followed our king behind,   somers = pack horse]
Till they came to green wood,
A mile under the lynde.   [lynde = linden trees]

There they met with good Robin,
Standing on the way,
And so did many a bold archer,
For sooth as I you say.

Robin took the king's horse,
Hastily in that stead,
And said, "Sir abbot, by your leave,
A while ye must abide.

"We be yeomen of this forest,
Under the green wood tree;
We live by our king's deer,
Under the green wood tree.

"And ye have churches and rents both,
And gold full great plenty;
Give us some of your spending,
For saint charity."   [saint = holy]

Than bespake our comely king,
Anon then said he: [anon = soon]
"I brought no more to green wood
But forty pound with me.

"I have lain at Nottingham
This fortnight with our king,
And spent I have full much good,
On many a great lording.

"And I have but forty pound,
No more than have I me;
But if I had an hundred pound,

I vouch it half on thee."

Robin took the forty pound,
And departed it in two party;   [departed = divided, party = parts]
Halfendell he gave his merry men,   [halfendell = half]
And bade them merry to be.

Full courteously Robin gan say;
"Sir, have this for your spending;
We shall meet another day."
"Gramercy," than said our king.   [gramercy = many thanks]

"But well thee greeteth Edward, our king,   [thee greeteth Edward
And sent to thee his seal,   = Edward greets you]
And biddeth thee come to Nottingham,
Both to meat and meal."

He took out the broad targe,   [targe = king's seal]
And soon he let him see;
Robin could his courtesy,   [his courtesy = act courteously]
And set him on his knee.

"I love no man in all the world
So well as I do my king;
Welcome is my lord's seal;
And, monk, for thy tiding,

"Sir abbot, for thy tidings,
To day thou shalt dine with me,
For the love of my king,
Under my trystell-tree."   [trystell = meeting]

Forth he led our comely king,
Full fair by the hand;
Many a deer there was slain,
And full fast dightand.   [dightand = prepared]

Robin took a full great horn,

And loud he gan blow;
Seven score of wight young men   [wight = strong]
Came ready on a row.

All they kneeled on their knee,
Full fair before Robin;
The king said him self until,   [him self until = to himself]
And swore by Saint Austin,   [Austin = Augustine]

"Here is a wonder seemly sight;
Me thinketh, by God's pine,   [pine = pain]
His men are more at his bidding
Then my men be at mine."

Full hastily was their dinner ydight,   [ydight = prepared]
And thereto gan they gone;   [gone = to go]
They served our king with all their might,
Both Robin and Little John.

Anon before our king was set   [anon = soon]
The fat venison,
The good white bread, the good red wine,
And thereto the fine ale and brown.

"Make good cheer," said Robin,
"Abbot, for charity,
And for this ilke tiding,   [ilke = same]
Blessed mote thou be.   [mote = may]

"Now shalt thou see what life we lead,
Ere thou hence wend;   [wend = go]
Then thou may inform our king,
When ye together lende."   [lende = dwell]

Up they stert all in haste,   [stert = started]
Their bows were smartly bent;
Our king was never so sore agast,   [agast = afraid]
He wend to have be shente.   [shente = killed]

Two yerdes there were up set,   [yerdes = rods, up set = set up]
Thereto gan they gang;   [gang = to go]
By fifty pace, our king said,
The marks were too long.*

On every side a rose-garland,
They shot under the line;
"Who so faileth of the rose-garland," said Robin,
"His tackle he shall tyne,   [tyne = forfeit]

"And yield it to his master,
Be it never so fine;
For no man will I spare,
So drink I ale or wine:

"And bear a buffet on his head,
Ywis right all bare."   [ywis = indeed]
And all that fell in Robin's lot,   [in Robin's lot = for Robin to strike]
He smote them wonder sore.

Twice Robin shot a bout,
And ever he cleaved the wand,
And so did good Gilbert
With the White Hand.

Little John and good Scathlock,
For nothing would they spare;
When they failed of the garland,
Robin smote them full sore.

At the last shot that Robin shot,
For all his friends fair,
Yet he failed of the garland,
Three fingers and more.

Than bespake good Gilbert,

---

* The king thought the targets were too far away to hit.

And thus he gan say:
"Master," he said, "your tackle is lost,
Stand forth and take your pay."

"If it be so," said Robin,
"That may no better be,
Sir abbot, I deliver thee mine arrow,
I pray thee, sir, serve thou me."

"It falleth not for mine order," said our king,
"Robin, by thy leave,
For to smite no good yeoman,
For doubt I should him grieve."

"Smite on boldly," said Robin,
"I give the large leave."
Anon our king, with that word,   [anon = soon]
He fold up his sleeve,

And such a buffet he gave Robin,
To ground he yede full near: [yede = went]
"I make mine avow to God," said Robin,
"Thou art a stalwart frere.   [frere = monk]

"There is pith in thine arm," said Robin,
"I trow thou canst well shoot."
Thus our king and Robin Hood
Together gan they meet.

Robin beheld our comely king
Wistly in the face,   [wistly = knowingly]
So did Sir Richard at the Lee,
And kneeled down in that place.

And so did all the wild outlaws,
When they see them kneel:
"My lord the king of England,
Now I know you well."

There is Pith in your arm said ROBIN HOOD

"Mercy then, Robin," said our king,   [mercy = thanks]
"Under your trystyll-tree,
Of thy goodness and thy grace,
For my men and me!"

"Yes, for God," said Robin,
"And also God me save,
I ask mercy, my lord the king,
And for my men I crave."

"Yes, for God," then said our king,
"And thereto sent I me,
With that thou leave the green wood,
And all thy company,

"And come home, sir, to my court,
And there dwell with me."
"I make mine avow to God," said Robin,
"And right so shall it be.

"I will come to your court,
Your service for to see,
And bring with me of my men
Seven score and three.

"But me like well your service,   [but me like = unless I like]
"I come again full soon,
And shoot at the dun deer,   [dun = tan]
As I am wont to doone."   [to doone = to do]

Fitt 8

"Hast thou any green cloth," said our king,
"That thou wilt sell now to me?"
"Yea, for God," said Robin,
"Thirty yards and three."

"Robin," said our king,
"Now pray I thee,
Sell me some of that cloth,
To me and my meyné."   [meyné = company]

"Yes, for God," then said Robin,
"Or else I were a fool:
Another day ye will me clothe,
I trow, against the Yule."   [against the Yule = for Christmas]

The king cast off his cowl then,
A green garment he did on,
And every knight had so, ywis,   [ywis = indeed]
Another hood full soon.   [another hood = different clothing]

When they were clothed in Lincoln green,
They cast away their gray:
"Now we shall to Nottingham,"
All thus our king gan say.

Their bows bent, and forth they went,
Shooting all in fere,   [in fere = together]
Toward the town of Nottingham,
Outlaws as they were.

Our king and Robin rode together,
For sooth as I you say,
And they shot plucke buffet,   [plucke buffet = with a buffet as the wager]
As they went by the way.

And many a buffet our king won
Of Robin Hood that day,
And nothing spared good Robin
Our king in his pay.

"So God me help," said our king,
"Thy game is naught to lere;   [lere = learn]
I should not get a shot of thee,

Though I shot all this year."

All the people of Nottingham
They stood and beheld;
They saw nothing but mantels of green
That covered all the field.

Than every man to other gan say,
"I dread our king be slain:
Come Robin Hood to the town, ywis   [ywis = indeed]
On live he left never one."   [on live = alive]

Full hastily they began to flee,
Both yeomen and knaves,
And old wives that might evil go,   [evil go = walk badly]
They hopped on their staves.

The king laugh full fast,
And commanded them again;
When they see our comely king,
I wis they were full fain.   [wis = know; fain = glad]

They ate and drank and made them glad,
And sang with notes high;
Than bespake our comely king
To Sir Richard at the Lee.

He gave him there his land again,
A good man he bade him be;
Robin thanked our comely king,
And set him on his knee.

Had Robin dwelled in the kings court
But twelve months and three,
That he had spent an hundred pound,
And all his men's fee.

In every place where Robin came

Ever more he laid down,   [laid down = gave money]
Both for knights and for squires,
To get him great renown.

By then the year was all agone
He had no man but twain,
Little John and good Scathlock,
With him all for to gone.   [to gone = to go]

Robin saw young men shoot
Full far upon a day;
"Alas!" then said good Robin,
"My wealth is went away.

"Sometime I was an archer good,
A stiff and eke a strong;   [stiff = steadfast, eke = also]
I was counted the best archer
That was in merry England.

"Alas!" then said good Robin,
"Alas and well a woe!
If I dwell longer with the king,
Sorrow will me slo."   [slo = slay]

Forth then went Robin Hood
Till he came to our king:
"My lord the king of England,
Grant me mine asking.

"I made a chapel in Barnesdale,
That seemly is to see,
It is of Mary Magdalene,
And thereto would I be.

"I might never in this seven night
No time to sleep ne wink,
Neither all these seven days
Neither eat ne drink.

"Me longeth sore to Barnesdale,
I may not be therefro;   [therefro = away from there]
Barefoot and woolward I have hight   [woolward = wearing wool
Thither for to go."   against the skin, hight = vowed]

"If it be so," then said our king,
"It may no better be,
Seven night I give thee leave,
No longer, to dwell fro me."   [fro = away from]

"Gramercy, lord," then said Robin,   [gramercy = many thanks]
And set him on his knee;
He took his leave courteously,
To green wood then went he.

When he came to green wood,
In a merry morning,
There he heard the notes small
Of birds merry singing.

"It is far gone," said Robin,
"That I was last here;
Me lyste a little for to shoot   [me lyste = I want]
At the dun deer."   [dun = tan]

Robin slew a full great hart,
His horn then gan he blow,
That all the outlaws of that forest
That horn could they know,

And gathered them together,
In a little throwe;   [throwe = while]
Seven score of wight young men   [wight = strong]
Came ready on a row.

And fair did of their hoods,
And set them on their knee:
"Welcome," they said, "our master,

Under this green wood tree."

Robin dwelled in green wood,
Twenty year and two;
For all dread of Edward our king,   [for all dread = although he feared]
Again would he not go.

Yet he was beguiled, ywis,   [ywis = indeed]
Through a wicked woman,
The prioress of Kirkely,
That nigh was of his kin,

For the love of a knight,
Sir Roger of Doncaster,
That was her own special;   [special = favorite]
Full evil mote they the!   [may they do very badly]

They took together their counsel
Robin Hood for to slay,
And how they might best do that deed,
His banis for to be.   [banis = murderers]

Than bespake good Robin,
In place where as he stood,
"To-morrow I must to Kirkely,
Craftily to be letten blood."   [craftily = skillfully, be letten blood
                                    = be bled, a medical treatment]

Sir Roger of Doncaster,
By the prioress he lay,
And there they betrayed good Robin Hood,
Through their false play.

Christ have mercy on his soul,
That died on the Rood!   [rood = cross]
For he was a good outlaw,
And did poor men much good.

Plays

The Merry Friar carrieth
Robin across the Water

Robin Hood and the Friar

This is the one early Robin Hood play that survives intact. It has a familiar plot: Robin Hood fights with someone, and when he sees how well he fights, he offers to take him into his band of men.

As it begins, Robin Hood complains to his men that a friar fought with him and robbed him. Friar Tuck comes to the forest and meets Robin Hood, who orders the friar to carry him across the river. The friar begins to carry him and then drops him in the river. They fight. Robin and Friar Tuck both call their men to help. After fighting, Robin offers to make Friar Tuck one of his men and to give him gold and a woman. The friar is happy to see the trollop that Robin Hood offers "to serve a friar at his lust."

The bawdy ending is the one feature of May plays that we do not find in the ballads.

This play survives because the printer William Copland added it to his edition of A Mery Geste of Robyn Hood and of Hys Lyfe, printed in about 1560. No manuscript version survives.

Here beginneth the Play of Robin Hood, very proper to be played in May Games

Scene 1:
Robin Hood and his men

Robin Hood:
Now stand ye forth my merry men all,
And hark what I shall say;
Of an adventure I shall you tell,

The which befell this other day.
As I went by the high way,
With a stout frere I met,   [frere = friar, monk]
And a quarter staff in his hand.
Lightly to me he lept,
And still he bade me stand.
There were stripes two or three,   [stripes = blows]
But I cannot tell who had the worse;
But well I wote the whoreson leaped within me   [wote = knew,
And from me he took my purse.   within = toward]
Is there any of my merry men all
That to that frere will go,
And bring him to me forth withall,
Whether he will or no?

Little John:
Yes, master, I make God avow,
To that frere will I go,
And bring him to you,
Whether he will or no.

Scene 2:
Friar Tuck, people and dogs on the road to the forest

Friar Tuck
Deus hic! Deus hic! God be here!
Is not this a holy word for a frere?
God save all this company!
But am not I a jolly friar?
For I can shoot both far and near,
And handle the sword and buckler,   [buckler = small shield]
And this quarter staff also.
If I meet with a gentleman or yeoman,
I am not afraid to look him upon,
Nor boldly with him to carp;   [carp = speak]
If he speak any words to me,
He shall have stripes two or three,
That shall make his body smart.
But, master, to show you the matter

Wherefore and why I am come hither,
In faith I will not spare,
I am come to seek a good yeoman,
In Barnesdale men say is his habitation.
His name is Robin Hood,
And if that he be better man than I,
His servant will I be, and serve him truly;
But if that I be better man than he,
By my truth my knave shall he be,
And lead these dogs all three.
God be here!;

Scene 3:
Robin Hood and Friar Tuck

Robin Hood:
Yield thee, friar, in thy long coat.

Friar Tuck:
I beshrew thy heart, knave, thou hurtest my throat. [beshrew = curse]

Robin Hood:
I trow, friar, thou beginnest to dote: [trow = think, dote = be foolish]
Who made thee so malapert and so bold   [malapert = rude]
To come into this forest here
Among my fallow deer?

Friar Tuck:
Go louse thee, ragged knave.   [louse thee = delouse yourself]
If thou make many words,
I will give thee on the ear,
Though I be but a poor friar.
To seek Robin Hood I am come here,
And to him my heart to breke.   [heart to breke = to reveal my feelings]

Robin Hood:
Thou lousy frere, what wouldest thou with him?
He never loved friar nor none of friar's kin.

Friar Tuck:
Avaunt, ye ragged knave!   [avaunt = away]
Or ye shall have on the skin.

Robin Hood:
Of all the men in the morning thou art the worst,
To meet with thee I have no lust;   [lust = desire]
For he that meeteth a frere or a fox in the morning,
To speed ill that day he standeth in jeopardy.   [speed ill = do badly]
Therefore I had liever meet with the devil of hell,   [liever = rather]
Friar, I tell thee as I think,
Then meet with a friar or a fox
In a morning, ere I drink.

Friar Tuck:
Avaunt, thou ragged knave, this is but a mock!
If you make many words, you shall have a knock.

Robin Hood:
Hark, frere, what I say here;
Over this water thou shalt me bear;
The bridge is borne away.

Friar Tuck:
To say nay I will not,   [let thee of = hinder you from
To let thee of thine oath, it were great pity and sin;   performing]
But upon a friar's back and have even in.   [but upon = but get up on]

Robin Hood:
Nay, have over.   [have over = go over the river]

Friar Tuck
Now am I, frere, within, and, thou, Robin, without,
To lay thee here I have no great doubt.
[Friar Tuck drops Robin Hood into the river.]
Now art thou, Robin, without, and I, frere, within,
Lie there, knave; chose whether thou wilt sink or swim.

Robin Hood:
Why, thou lousy frere, what hast thou done?

Friar Tuck:
Mary, set a knave over the shoon.*   [shoon = shoes]

Robin Hood:
Therefore thou abye.   [abye = bear the consequences]

Friar Tuck:
Why, wilt thou fight a pluck?   [pluck = fight with staves]

Robin Hood:
And God send me good luck.

Friar Tuck:
Than have a stroke for Friar Tuck.   [for = from]

[They fight.]

Robin Hood:
Hold thy hand, frere, and hear me speak.

Friar Tuck:
Say on, ragged knave,
Me seemeth ye begin to sweat.

Robin Hood:
In this forest I have a hound,
I will not give him for an hundred pound:
Give me leave my horn to blow,
That my hound may know.

Friar Tuck:
Blow on, ragged knave, without any doubt,
Until both thine eyes start out.

Scene 4:
Robin Hood's men enter after he blows his horn

Friar Tuck:
Here be a sort of ragged knaves come in,
Clothed all in Kendale green,
And to thee they take their way now.

* Turned a knave head over heels.

Robin Hood:
Peradventure they do so.   [peradventure = perhaps]

Friar Tuck:
I gave the leave to blow at thy will;
Now give me leave to whistle my fill.

Robin Hood:
Whistle, frere, evil mote thou fare! [evil mote thou fare = may you do badly]
Until both thine eyes start.

Scene 5:
Friar Tuck's Men enter after he whistles

Friar Tuck:
Now Cut and Bause!   [Cut and Bause = names of his men]
Bring forth the clubs and staves,
And down with those ragged knaves.

[They fight.]

Robin Hood:
How sayest thou, frere, wilt thou be my man,
To do me the best service thou can?
Thou shalt have both gold and fee.
And also here is a lady free:
[A lady enters.]
I will give her unto thee,
And her chaplain I thee make
To serve her for my sake.

Friar Tuck:
Here is an huckle duckle,
An inch above the buckle.
She is a trull of trust,   [trull = trollop]
To serve a friar at his lust,
A pricker, a prancer, a tearer of sheets,
A wagger of ballocks when other men sleeps.
Go home, ye knaves, and lay crabbs in the fire,   [crabbs = trivets]
For my lady and I will dance in the mire,

Robin Hood and the Potter

The printer William Copland added this fragment of a play it to his edition of "A Mery Geste of Robyn Hood and of Hys Lyfe," as if it were a continuation of the play Robin Hood and the Friar.

It is only a brief fragment, telling the beginning of the story that we have in the ballad Robin Hood and the Potter. Based on that ballad, we can assume that the play continued with the potter beating Robin Hood, the two becoming friends, and Robin Hood taking the pots to Nottingham and using them to trick the sheriff.

We can speculate about the play's ending. In the ballad, Robin Hood gives the sheriff's wife gifts, and the play concludes with her laughing at the sheriff when he tells her how he was tricked. In the ballad, it looks like an example of Robin's gallantry to women, which the ballads say is caused by his devotion of Mary, but in a May play, we expect a bawdy ending, like that of Robin Hood and the Friar. Could it be that, at the end of the play, the audience learned that Robin Hood gave her gifts because she had sex with him, cuckolding the sheriff? The play begins with Robin calling the potter a cuckold, so it would not be surprising if it ended with Robin calling the sheriff a cuckold.

Scene 1:
Robin Hood and his men

Robin Hood:
Listen to me my merry men all
And hark what I shall say
Of an adventure I shall you tell
That befell this other day.

With a proud potter I met;
And a rose garland on his head,
The flowers of it shone marvelous fresh.   [shone = showed, appeared]
This seven year and more he hath used this way,
Yet was he never so courteous a potter
As one penny passage to pay.
Is there any of my merry men all
That dare be so bold
To make the potter pay passage either silver or gold?

Little John:

Not I, master, for twenty pound ready told.   [told = counted]
For there is not among us all one
That dare meddle with that potter man for man.
I felt his hands not long agone,   [agone = ago]
But I had lever have been here by thee.   [lever = rather]
Therefore I know what he is;
Meet him when ye will or meet him when ye shall
He is as proper a man as ever you meddle withal.   [meddle withal = fought with]

Robin Hood:

I will lay with thee, Little John, twenty pound so red,   [lay = bet]
If I with that potter meet
I will make him pay passage, maugré his head.   [maugré his head = despite his will]

Little John

I consent thereto, so eat I bread;
If he pay passage, maugré his head,
Twenty pound shall ye have of me for your mede. [mede = reward]

Scene 2:
Robin Hood and Jack the potter's boy

Jack:

Out alas that ever I saw this day!
For I am clean out of my way
From Nottingham town.
If I hie me not the faster,   [hie = hurry]
Ere I come there the market will be done.

Robin Hood:

Let me see, are the pots whole and sound?
[Robin Hood takes a pot and throws it on the ground.]

Jack:

Yea, master, but they will not break the ground.

Robin Hood:

I will them break for the cuckold thy master's sake;
And if they will break the ground,
Thou shalt have three pence for a pound.
[Robin Hood breaks more pots.]

Jack:

Out alas! What have ye done?
If my master come, he will break your crown.

Scene 3:
The potter enters, joining Robin Hood and Jack

Potter:

Why, thou whoreson, art thou here yet?
Thou shouldst have been at market.

Jack:

I met with Robin Hood, a good yeoman;
He hath broken my pots,
And called you cuckold by your name.

Potter:

Thou mayst be a gentleman, so God me save,
But thou seemest a naughty knave.
Thou callest me cuckold by my name,
And I swear by God and Saint John,
Wife had I never none:
But if thou be a good fellow,
I will sell my horse, my harness, pots and panniers too,
Thou shalt have the one half, and I will have the other.
If thou be not so content,

Thou shalt have stripes, if thou were my brother.*

Robin Hood:
Hark, potter, what I shall say;
This seven year and more thou hast used this way,
Yet were thou never courteous to me
As one penny passage to pay.

Potter:
Why should I pay passage to thee?

Robin Hood:
For I am Robin Hood, chief governor
Under the green wood tree.

Potter:
This seven year have I used this way up and down,
Yet paid I passage to no man;
Nor now I will not begin, to do the worst thou can.

Robin Hood:
Passage shalt thou pay, here under the green wood tree,
Or else thou shalt leave a wedded with me.   [wedded = forfeit]

Potter:
If thou be a good fellow, as men do thee call,
Lay away thy bow,
And take thy sword and buckler in thy hand,
And see what shall befall.

Robin Hood:
Little John, where art thou?

Little John:
Here, master, I make God avow.
I told you, master, so God me save,
That you should find the potter a knave.

---

* The potter offers to pay Robin half of his goods as a compromise, which is not consistent with his refusal to pay anything. These four lines probably come from another story, where someone who was being robbed offered to compromise with Robin, and were added here by mistake.

Hold your buckler in your hand,
And I will stiffly by you stand,   [stiffly = steadfastly]
Ready for to fight;
Be the knave never so stout,
I shall rap him on the snout,
And put him to flight.

[The rest of the text is missing.]

ROBIN. and. LITTLE. JOHN. go. their. ways. in.
search. of. Adventure: